Battle Orders • 19

The US Marine Corps in the Vietnam War

III Marine Amphibious Force 1965–75

Ed Gilbert

Consultant Editor Dr Duncan Anderson • *Series editors* Marcus Cowper and Nikolai Bogdanovic

First published in Great Britain in 2006 by Osprey Publishing, Midland House, West Way,
Botley, Oxford OX2 0PH, United Kingdom.
Email: info@ospreypublishing.com

ISBN 1 84176 987 8

Page layout by Bounford.com, Royston, UK
Maps by Bounford.com, Royston, UK
Typeset in Stone Serif and GillSans
Index by Alan Thatcher
Originated by PPS Grasmere Ltd, Leeds, UK
Printed and bound in China by Bookbuilders

06 07 08 09 10   10 9 8 7 6 5 4 3 2 1

A CIP catalog record for this book is available from the British Library.

For a catalog of all books published by Osprey Military and Aviation please contact:
Osprey Direct USA, c/o Random House Distribution Center, 400 Hahn Rd,
Westminster, MD 21157 USA
E-mail: info@ospreydirect.com

Osprey Direct UK, P.O. Box 140, Wellingborough, Northants, NN8 2FA, UK
E-mail: info@ospreydirect.co.uk

www.ospreypublishing.com

Image credits

The photographic images that appear in this work were obtained
from the National Archives and Records Administration and the
Marine Corps Research Center, MCB Quantico. The author would
like to acknowledge the assistance of Bob Acquilina, Charles
Melson (Major, USMC, ret.) and Dieter Stenger of the History
and Museums Branch, the staff of the Archives Section, Marine
Corps Research Center, Col. Joe Sleger (USMC, ret.), and Lt.
Col. Ken Estes (USMC, ret.).

Author's note

Standard Marine Corps terminology has been used throughout
this volume. **Dates** are stated in the form day/month/year. **Unit
designations** reflect Marine practice; 1/4 refers to 1st Battalion,
4th Marines. Marine regiments are not separately identified as
infantry or artillery as in Army practice. The term "Marines" always
refers to a regiment, as opposed to "Marine Division." Since World
War II the 1st Marine Division has included the 1st, 5th and 7th
Marines (infantry), and 11th Marines (artillery). The 3rd Marine
Division includes the 3rd, 4th, and 9th Marines (infantry) and 12th
Marines (artillery). Other organic division units such as Engineer,
Shore Party, Antitank and Tank battalions usually carry the same
number as the division. **Map and unit tree symbols** are also
depicted with standard Marine symbols. Note that on maps,
USMC units are indicated in olive green, Army of the Republic
of Vietnam (ARVN) in blue, and Communist forces and positions
in red. For a key to the symbols used in this volume, see below.

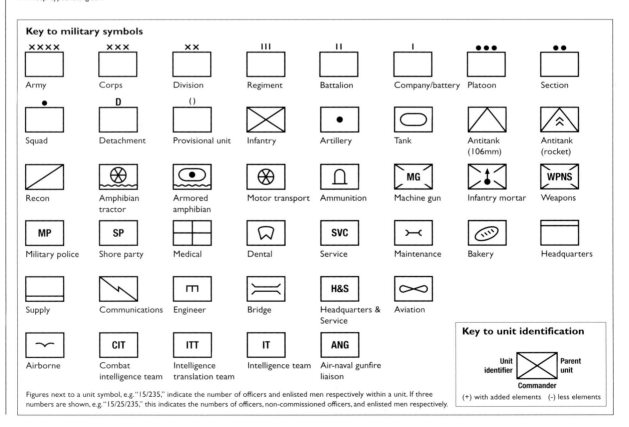

Contents

Introduction

The war in the five northern provinces of the Republic of Vietnam – the I Corps operational area – combined both guerrilla and conventional combat, as the US Marine Corps fought both Viet Cong (VC) guerrillas and the regular forces of the North Vietnamese Army (NVA). This study will cover the organization and evolution of the Marine Corps ground forces in Vietnam by examining the overall multi-division corps command structure, III Marine Amphibious Force (III MAF).

The struggle against the local VC guerrilla forces was in principle familiar to the Marines from long experience as America's "colonial infantry." Platoons or squads of the Combined Action Program (CAP), in coordination with local militias, fought for control of the "hearts and minds" of the rural peasantry.

I Corps' tactical area of responsibility.

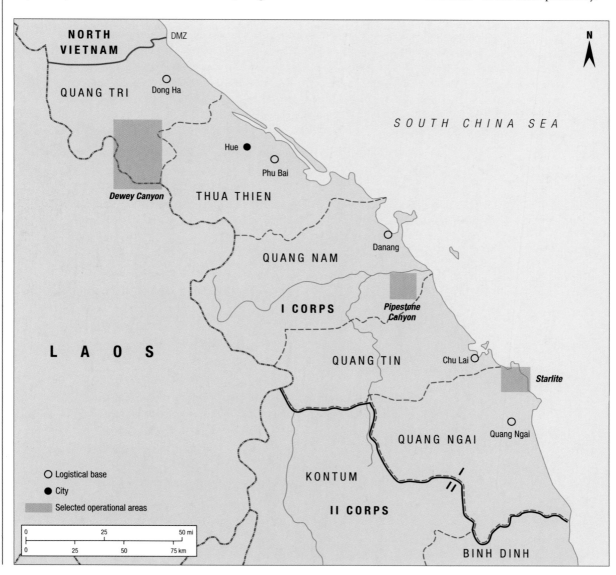

The conventional war against the VC Main Force battalions and the regiments and divisions of the NVA was unlike anything from the Marine Corps' institutional experience. With few exceptions the Marines had previously fought as integrated divisions or multi-division Amphibious Corps. Vietnam provided limited scope for the amphibious assaults that were the specialty of the Marines.

While the division remained the fundamental unit of Marine Corps organization, *ad hoc* brigade task forces conducted the "campaigns" of the Vietnam War. These brigades were often made up of companies or battalions

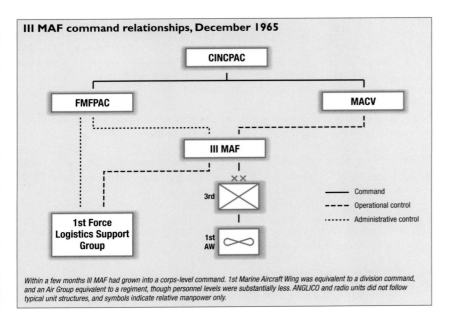

III MAF command relationships, December 1965

Within a few months III MAF had grown into a corps-level command. 1st Marine Aircraft Wing was equivalent to a division command, and an Air Group equivalent to a regiment, though personnel levels were substantially less. ANGLICO and radio units did not follow typical unit structures, and symbols indicate relative manpower only.

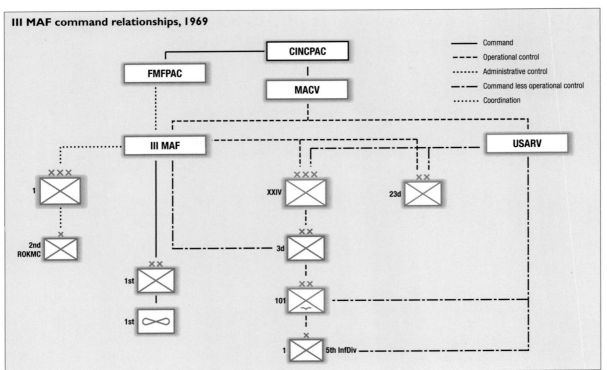

III MAF command relationships, 1969

from different regiments or even different divisions, and the composition was constantly changing. Units within the country were in constant flux as forces were built up or reduced, organizational structures changed, and units moved in and out of the country as forces were modified, or simply for recuperation. Finally, the command structures of units changed with stunning rapidity as officers were rotated through command billets at all levels.

Other command structures outside the divisions played critical roles in the conflict. Two such organizations were the small units of the CAP that fought the anti-guerrilla campaign at the village and hamlet level, and Force Logistics Command (FLC) that supported all ground and air combat elements.

The Vietnam War was also unique for the Marine Corps as for the first time a "deep" logistical support structure fell under a field corps command, and was a vital part of the organization. The logistical support organization that evolved was a military oddity that did not follow the usual hierarchical structure. FLC was operationally under III MAF, but administratively under a higher command, Fleet Marine Forces Pacific (FMFPAC). At the lower end the Logistical Support Unit (LSU) that supported each regiment in the field might be answerable to four or more "parent" units. This structure sometimes baffles even veterans.

An added complexity was III MAF's relationships with other commands. At times III MAF units might be under the operational control of an Army corps, though under administrative control of III MAF. Similarly, Army and some allied units such as the Republic of Korea Marine Corps Brigade and units of the Army of the Republic of Vietnam (ARVN) were under the operational control of III MAF.

The complexity, and moreover the weekly changes in the structure of Marine Corps forces in Vietnam, would be impossible to capture in 20 or more works of this size. The structure of III MAF and its component units will be examined as a series of "snapshots" at key points in time. A few of the hundreds of combat operations will be examined only as they reveal key aspects of the Task Forces that typically carried out such operations. No detailed command chronologies will be presented, since numerous officers occupied the same command billet over the course of the war.

The origins of III Marine Amphibious Force

The origins of III MAF reflect the incremental nature of US involvement in Vietnam, and the political sensitivities of the era. As the American commitment to the defense of South Vietnam grew, by early 1965 it was apparent that US forces would grow beyond the handful of Army advisors, and the Army and Marine Corps aviation units, already present. The Communist attack against the airbase at Pleiku in the early morning hours of 7 February prompted immediate retaliatory air strikes against North Vietnam, which raised concerns that the North Vietnamese might retaliate in kind. The Marine Corps' Battery A, 1st Light Anti-Aircraft Missile (LAAM) Battalion, was assigned to defend the facilities around Danang. Following some brief confusion about air transport, the battery was set up and ready to fire within 12 hours of arrival, on 8 February.

Concerned by both the northern threat and civil unrest inside South Vietnam, in late February President Johnson decided to commit major ground combat elements. This triggered a debate about whether to deploy the Army's 173rd Airborne Brigade, or Marines. The 9th Marine Expeditionary Brigade (drawn from the 3rd Division, and under the command of the Assistant Division Commander, Brigadier General Frederick Karch) was chosen largely because their organic logistical support made them more self-sustaining. Naval Task Force 76 landed 3rd Battalion, 9th Marines over the beach on the morning of 8 March, and 1st Battalion, 3rd Marines followed by air the same day. The force carried rations and ammunition for 15 days.

By 22 March the logistical tail (elements of 3rd Service Battalion and Force Service Regiment, Okinawa), as well as an additional Marine Air Group (MAG-16 also assumed responsibility for 1st LAAM Battalion), were in the country. At this point the ground forces amounted to an Expeditionary Brigade, but with the added complexity of two Marine Air Groups and logistical units. On 5 May the Joint Chiefs of Staff approved a "force/division/wing headquarters to include Commanding General 3rd Marine Division and 1st Marine Aircraft Wing." Such a division-scale composite unit would be designated a Marine Expeditionary Force (MEF) under the Corps' naming practices. Major General William R. "Rip" Collins, who had commanded 6th Tank Battalion on Okinawa in 1945, established III MEF. This precipitated an immediate political problem.

The South Vietnamese government and the American embassy were anxious to downplay the American combat presence because the South Vietnamese populace was in a state of near rebellion. The title of the new unit carried an unpleasant similarity to the colonialist French Expeditionary Corps of the 1950s, which was bound to further inflame Vietnamese nationalists of every political stripe. Marine Commandant Wallace M. Greene Jr. selected the name "Amphibious Force" because it avoided the politically charged words "Expeditionary" and "Corps," and harkened back to the "Amphibious Corps" terminology of the Pacific War.

This force eventually assumed the scale of a multi-divisional, corps-level command, but because of political sensitivities retained the "Force," or reinforced divisional command, designation.

The HAWK missile batteries of 1st LAAM were deployed to protect against a potential North Vietnamese air attack. The ground troops assigned to protect the missile batteries and air base at Danang set the stage for the massive American intervention. After III MAF was organized, the missile batteries passed to operational control of 1st Marine Aircraft Wing. These missiles are overlooking Dodge City, a base 19km west of Danang. (NARA)

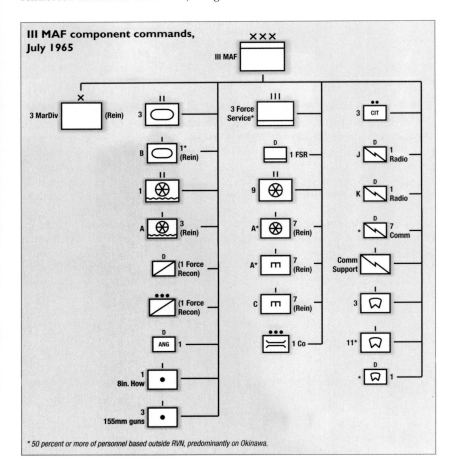

III MAF component commands, July 1965

* 50 percent or more of personnel based outside RVN, predominantly on Okinawa.

Combat mission

In 1965 the United States Marine Corps was a force of three active-duty divisions and a reserve division, with one of the most ambitious missions ever assigned to a military force. Each division functioned primarily as light infantry, but with powerful and permanently integrated components including a regiment of artillery and logistics and support units. Additional heavy components such as a tank battalion, an amphibian tractor battalion, and independent heavy artillery batteries, were held at Force Troops (corps) level but were integrated into the division both in doctrine and training. Unlike Army units of comparable scale, it was an all-arms, stand-alone unit, capable of sustaining itself and fighting far from bases or external support. In addition, each division was laterally integrated with a supporting air wing, with both fixed wing and helicopter units specifically trained to support "their" ground forces.

Units assigned from corps level also supported Army divisions, but units within the Marine division handled division support functions such as logistics, heavy engineer, and specialized ordnance repair.

The Corps' mission was ambitious and diverse. In a conventional war the Marines might have to spearhead an amphibious assault to seize airfields or seaports, and block the advance of Soviet mechanized forces until the arrival of more heavily equipped Army divisions. In this role they had to be ready to deploy brigades or divisions anywhere from northern Norway, around the margin of Europe, through Turkey and into the Persian Gulf. A more common role was to defend American military, political, or economic interests by

Force Troops artillery units were equipped with M55 8in. howitzers like "BIGFOOT," and M53 155mm guns. These big guns saw service in Vietnam as independent batteries, assigned to artillery regiments or to the Field Artillery Group. They were eventually replaced in service by the more familiar M110 8in. howitzer and M107 175mm gun. (NARA)

landing battalion-sized forces virtually anywhere in the world to suppress local fighting, evacuate or protect American and other friendly nationals, and act as peacekeepers. Some typical examples among dozens of Marine Corps interventions were a landing, at the request of the Lebanese government, to forestall a possible Syrian invasion (1958), and to end civil war in the Dominican Republic (1965). The Marines also helped evacuate foreign nationals during an Indonesian civil war (1957–58), stood ready to defend Taiwan against a Communist Chinese invasion (1958), and evacuated foreign nationals from various Latin American countries. In all these cases the Marine landing forces had to contend not only with hostile military forces, but irregular or guerrilla forces as well.

A further role was a humanitarian one: to establish order and, through its organic logistics and engineering services, provide relief in the aftermath of natural disasters such as storms and earthquakes.

This organizational structure and diverse mission was as much a product of politics as of military struggle and accomplishment. Within four months of its founding in November 1775 the Corps had conducted its first amphibious landing, on New Providence Island in the Bahamas. A battalion of Marines distinguished themselves in land combat at the Battle of Bladensburg, a failed effort to defend the city of Washington against a British raid in August 1814. For most of its history, though, the Corps served as an adjunct security force to the Navy, and conducted expeditionary landings and raids.

In 1917 a Marine brigade fought as part of the US Army's 2nd Division, over the objections of the revered commander of the American Expeditionary Force, General John Pershing. By a vagary of the AEF publicity policy – and its efficient and courageous performance in the battle for Belleau Wood – the Brigade won public acclaim while Army units who fought alongside felt they had been slighted. This set the stage for acrimony and rivalry that lasted for nearly a century.

As military budgets shrank after the Armistice of 1918, and searching for a role that did not duplicate that of the Army, General John A. Lejeune, Majors Earl H. Ellis and Holland M. Smith, and other "futurists" of the Corps developed a new doctrine of amphibious assault – attacking directly from the sea, as opposed to making an "administrative" landing and marching overland to battle. By 1945 the Corps had firmly established itself as America's amphibious assault specialists, and had evolved and expanded to six divisions, air wings of corresponding size, and numerous smaller specialist units.[1] In the post World War II era Army leaders, with the implicit backing of President Harry Truman, sought to limit both the size and influence of the Corps, which General of the Army Omar Bradley complained was a "second Army." This effort never achieved much, because Marine Corps advocates in Congress, and public opinion of the Corps, were bolstered by the superb performance of the Marines in resisting the Communist Chinese onslaught in Korea in December 1950. Truman sent his personal observer, Army Reserve Major General Frank E. Lowe (Lowe served with Truman in World War I) to Korea to evaluate the disaster that had befallen the Eighth Army and X Corps, which included the 1st Marine Division. Lowe wrote to Truman, "The First Marine Division is the most efficient and courageous combat unit that I have ever seen or heard of," and advocated the intensive Marine Corps style of training for all branches of the services.

In 1952 legislation established the Corps as a service separate from but still linked to the Navy, with its own specified roles and missions. A primary mission would be the seizure of advanced naval bases, but following World War II the seizure of advanced air bases achieved equal importance. The Corps would continue to be amphibious assault specialists, and to this was added the new tactic of vertical envelopment, or helicopter-borne assault. In theory the Marines would seize footholds on enemy territory by amphibious or helicopter

---

1 See Battle Orders 1, 7, and 8 on the USMC in World War II.

assault. Army formations would then take over to prosecute longer land campaigns. In World War II this ideal two-stage campaign seldom proved to be the case in actual practice. The Marines had engaged in lengthy land campaigns in the Pacific, and had to anticipate similar campaigns in any future war.

A second and very significant mission was to serve as a "force in readiness" for immediate deployment anywhere in the world, and to confront any type of military threat. To fulfill this mission the Corps designed a flexible organizational structure of all-arms teams with combat, support, and even air assets brigaded together. These were eventually formalized at battalion (Marine Expeditionary Unit, or MEU), regimental (Marine Expeditionary Brigade, or MEB) and division (Marine Expeditionary Force, or MEF) scale. A typical MEB, of which there were several constantly at sea, was built around a rifle battalion, supported by one or perhaps two artillery batteries, as well as platoons of tanks, antitank weapons, amphibian tractors, reconnaissance troops, trucks, engineers, medical personnel, shore party (beachhead management and unloading specialists), and small detachments of headquarters personnel, communications specialists, logistics specialists, and even a dental unit. Also embarked was a squadron of 20 to 24 helicopters. Escort vessels such as destroyers provided gunfire support, and Navy or Marine Corps fixed-wing air support would typically be available from an aircraft carrier battle group.

The Corps continued to experiment with new doctrines and technology that would prove critical in future struggles. The 1954 book *Cavalry of the Sky* described Marine helicopter operations in Korea, and a 1955 plan for a helicopter-borne division (never implemented because of inadequate funding) pre-dated the Army's air cavalry concept by a decade. A 1956 staff study concluded that there would likely be no nuclear war with the USSR, but a series of wars against Soviet proxies outside Europe. The Corps was reconfigured as a light infantry force to conduct airmobile or amphibious landings anywhere on the globe, but not all changes were for the better. Tank battalions, and both tube and rocket artillery, became Force Troops assets, and organic logistics capabilities were pared down. The standard divisional artillery piece was to be a wheeled 4.2in. mortar (the uniquely Marine Corps "Howtar"), and regimental mechanized antitank units were equipped with the air portable M50 Ontos.

In the late 1950s the Corps struggled once more against an Army initiative to assume the "force in readiness" role. The Corps held an advantage in that amphibious forces inevitably had more logistical "staying power" than the two airborne and two air-transported "leg infantry" divisions of the Strategic Army Corps (STRAC).

The appointment of a new commandant, General David Shoup, in 1960 and the installation of the new administration of President John Kennedy in 1961 led to an upturn in the Corps' fortunes and funding. The Corps' leadership was most pleased with the new Kennedy doctrine of "flexible response," meeting force with measured counterforce without immediately resorting to nuclear weapons.

The Corps and supporting naval units received funding for more amphibious shipping, a new generation of helicopters (the CH-47 Sea Knight and CH-53A Sea Stallion heavy-lift helicopter, though they were eventually forced to adopt the Army's UH-1) and fixed-wing aircraft (the F-4 Phantom II fighter-bomber, A-4 Skyhawk close-air support plane, and the A-6A Intruder all-weather bomber).

The Marine Corps leadership did not, however, share the new administration's infatuation with "special warfare." They did not view it as a separate mission, but considered counterinsurgency operations and similar small-unit campaigns as a natural extension of the "force in readiness" role. In fact, the Marines had literally written the book on counterinsurgency. *Small Wars Manual* was a 1940 compendium of lessons from campaigns in Haiti, the Dominican Republic, and the Philippines, and is still a seminal work in counterinsurgency warfare. Training in counter-guerrilla operations, even if limited and often unrealistic, was far better than that received by most Army units.

A cadre of veteran officers and NCOs, many of whom had served in both World War II and Korea, provided the senior leadership. As a fundamental part of their training, junior officers and enlisted men were indoctrinated with the history and traditions of the Corps. Because of the tradition of small independent landing parties, and the potential of organizational chaos posed by heavy casualties in an amphibious assault, initiative and leadership at junior levels was heavily emphasized. In short, Marines considered themselves an elite force.

Thus by the early 1960s the Corps' mission was to be jacks-of-all-trades, and masters of many. They were to stand ready to deploy to any part of the world, and to confront any threat with a counterforce of battalion to division scale. They had, in theory, to be prepared to land either as an amphibious force or a helicopter-borne assault force, or a combination. Once ashore, they might have to face Soviet mechanized forces in conventional warfare or quell an insurgency, prop up a friendly government, or provide disaster relief. In short, they were tasked to perform almost any conceivable mission.

Commandant Shoup summarized the combat mission in 1961. When the Marines were attacked by extreme right-wing members of Congress for being "soft on Communism," Shoup simply stated "We're professional soldiers. We fight any enemy the President designates." The Marines were the natural choice among forces to deploy to South Vietnam.

Marine divisions were made self-sustaining by inclusion of organic logistics units like the shore party battalion, whose responsibility was to unload, organize, and handle heavy cargo. This heavy all-terrain forklift of 3rd Shore Party Battalion is handling palletized ammunition at a regimental supply point in Vietnam. (MCRC)

Doctrine and training

The Marine Corps, by the nature of its history and missions, had been forced to develop a variety of doctrines, but for the latter part of the 20th century the major emphasis was always on amphibious assault doctrine. For the conflict in Vietnam, the two most relevant doctrines were those dealing with ground combat and counterinsurgency, and how they secondarily impacted on the doctrines of supporting arms.

Land combat doctrine

Marine Corps land combat doctrine was a direct outgrowth of its amphibious assault doctrine, developed in the 1930s and refined in the savage fighting of the Pacific War of 1941–45. It was, and remains, an offensive doctrine, emphasizing destruction of the enemy by rapid establishment of fire superiority, maneuver, and aggressive assault.

The Marines pioneered the new amphibious assault doctrine for the seizure of small-island objectives by frontal assault from the sea. This flew in the face of every established military principle in the post-World War I era, when the "strategy of the indirect approach" – seeking to outmaneuver the enemy, and above all avoid a frontal attack – reigned supreme.

Marine Corps planners analyzed many historical amphibious campaigns, and in particular the failures of the Gallipoli campaign. A basic Marine doctrinal principle would be to land a self-sufficient, all-arms force, with its own engineers, artillery, and tank support. The Marines had already experimented with using aircraft in tactical support of ground troops, and utilized aircraft and naval gunfire support as a substitute for heavy artillery.

The Marine Corps pioneered the doctrine of close air support, and emphasized the precision application of supporting fires. The Air-Naval Gunfire Liaison Company (ANGLICO) was trained and equipped to communicate with artillery, fixed-wing air support, and naval gunfire from destroyers, cruisers and battleships. This ANGLICO Team in Vietnam illustrates the special equipment used by the teams. (MCRC)

A second basic principle would be speed coupled with aggressive attack. In an amphibious assault, there is no option for withdrawal or lateral maneuver, only success or catastrophic failure, as acknowledged by General of the Army Dwight Eisenhower before the Normandy landings. The Marines felt that success could be best assured by fast-moving, aggressive assault in overpowering force, and acceptance of the inevitable casualties in achieving the mission. Greater immediate casualty rates actually minimized long-term losses. The more quickly the objective could be captured, the less the exposure of the vulnerable naval transports to enemy counterattack. This belief was vindicated by the Gilbert Islands campaign of November 1943. The 2nd Marine Division suffered 984 dead in three days of savage fighting to capture heavily fortified Tarawa Atoll and eliminate its 4,836 defenders. The Army's 27th Division fought slowly and systematically to eliminate the tiny garrison (300 combat troops and about 250 Korean laborers) of lightly defended Makin Atoll, with only 66 killed. But on the fourth day a Japanese submarine arrived at Makin and sank the aircraft carrier *Liscome Bay*, with the loss of 644 sailors.

The little-known New Georgia campaign was a test of the cherished indirect approach strategy. Rather than frontally attack the Japanese base at Munda, the 43rd Infantry Division landed five miles (8km) away, and launched a systematic overland approach. In three months of horrific jungle fighting, American and Allied troops lost 1,117 killed or missing, and 3,873 wounded. Additional losses included several naval vessels and numerous aircraft. It was the death knell of the indirect approach.

The Marines carried the lessons of the amphibious assault doctrine over into generalized land combat. Emphasis was upon defeat and destruction of the enemy by (1) establishing superiority of fire, and (2) direct infantry assault. Fire superiority was achieved by precision, not simply volume. Primary training placed great emphasis on individual marksmanship, and although aimed fire was often not achievable, habit minimized the temptation to "spray and pray." This doctrine also applied to supporting arms, where the emphasis was on the

The Marines conducted the first helicopter assault in September 1951, but budgetary constraints prevented the realization of the planned airmobile division. In the early days of the war older helicopters like the UH-34 were still the primary tactical examples. (MCRC)

The Corps emphasized an all-arms doctrine, but remained wedded to the concept of the tank as a dedicated infantry support weapon. Here an M67 flame tank and an M50A1 Ontos train with officer candidates at Quantico. (MCRC)

precise delivery of ordnance onto the target by artillery, naval gunfire, or aircraft in direct support of ground forces.

The primary task of all supporting assets, not just artillery, was immediate support of the infantry who would close with the enemy. Marine direct air support meant control of the attacking aircraft and their target selection by the men on the ground, and the placement of bombs or napalm in close proximity to ground troops – in some cases within tens of meters.

Marine doctrine also differed from that of the Army in two significant respects: the tactical use of helicopters, and of armor. Since the Marine doctrine of vertical envelopment was developed primarily for amphibious assault, heavy supporting fires for helicopter assaults were to be delivered by a combination of fixed-wing aircraft operating from aircraft carriers or naval guns (in Vietnam, largely replaced by land-based and air artillery respectively). The Marines entered the war with no dedicated helicopter gun ships like the "aerial rocket artillery" of the Army's 1st Air Cavalry, but in 1969 adopted the specially designed AH-1G "Cobra" gunship for escort and ground attack.

Helicopters replaced amphibian tractors as troop transports and logistics carriers, and so the most commonly used types were large-capacity troop carriers like the CH-46 Sea Knight. Slower, but with a far greater lift capacity than the smaller helicopters favored by the Army, these were suitable for quickly moving large numbers of troops off limited deck space of ships. The doctrine for employment of helicopters closely paralleled the doctrine for use of amphibian tractors developed in World War II. In Marine doctrine helicopters were "battle taxis," not assault vehicles.

Much to the frustration of the Corps' tank advocates, the Marines never developed a truly coherent armor doctrine. Though one of the Corps' primary missions was to stand ready to counter a potential Soviet mechanized onslaught, the Marines remained largely wedded to the concept of the infantry support tank. Doctrine called for the potential for mechanized operations in suitable conditions of open terrain, but no truly practical training or exercises were conducted. Uncharacteristically, anti-armor doctrine was largely defensive in scope.

The division tank battalions were organized with three companies of M48A3 main battle tanks and a single company of M103A2 heavy tanks. The heavy tanks were not used in Vietnam. In Vietnam armor assets were parceled out in platoons or even sections of two or three vehicles for infantry support, convoy escort, and even guard duty.[2] The few armored task forces that were organized were *ad hoc* affairs, like Task Force ROBBIE of the 3rd Marine Division along the Demilitarized Zone (DMZ). This mobile force included a Marine tank company and several infantry companies, two Army M42 self-propelled 40mm AAA guns, and two companies of Army gun trucks mounting quadruple .50-cal. machine guns in power turrets. Fortunately the Marines never faced a mechanized threat in Vietnam, but the "lessons" of the conflict further retarded development of a Marine armor doctrine.

Counterinsurgency doctrine

The Marines had extensive experience in combating guerrillas and insurgents dating back to the early 19th-century campaigns against the Creek and Seminole tribes of the southeastern United States. The Marine Corps' lengthy experiences in the Philippines Insurrection (1899–1902), the interventions in Haiti and the Dominican Republic (1915–34), and particularly the struggle against revolutionary forces in Nicaragua (1926–33) were crucial in the formulation of a counter-guerrilla doctrine as expressed in the *Small Wars Manual*. The lessons of Nicaragua were remarkably relevant, particularly the battles against highly organized and well-equipped guerrillas who moved in and out of "sanctuaries" across borders.

Marine doctrine was the mirror image of the doctrine followed by Communist forces. Before Chairman Mao dictated that the guerrillas were "fish that swam in the sea of the people," Marine doctrine had stressed achieving both physical and psychological separation of guerrillas from the people by treating non-combatants fairly, befriending the populace, and minimizing damage to people and property. In the words of the *Small Wars Manual*:

> The goal is to gain decisive results with the least application of force and the consequent minimum loss of life. The end aim is the social, economic, and political development of the people subsequent to the military defeat of the enemy insurgent forces. In small wars, tolerance, sympathy, and kindness should be the keynote of our relationship with the mass of the population.

The Marines considered pacification programs a primary task, and devoted considerable manpower and both charitable and financial assets to the programs. Sir Robert Thompson, a British expert in counterinsurgency warfare, reported that "[the] Marine Corps alone made a serious attempt to achieve permanent and lasting results … by seeking to protect the rural population." Under the CAP, squads of volunteers received training in Vietnamese culture and customs, then moved into a village to live, work, and fight alongside the local Vietnamese forces. Marine units provided medical care and training, built and supplied schools, conducted civic improvements such as agricultural programs and construction of water supplies, and provided clothing and food for refugees. A great part of this effort was supported by volunteer fund-raising activities of the Reserve components.

Training

The Marine Corps is sometimes called the world's largest elite force. The organization seeks to inculcate on a large scale the primary attributes of elite forces – not just individual courage, discipline, and devotion to mission, but

---

2 See Osprey Warrior 90, *US Marine Tank Crewman 1965–70.*

Marine "boot camp" was designed to not only instill pride and military skills, but to develop and preserve individual initiative rather than create compliant robots. To this end, training was surprisingly individualized. Family tradition was an important recruiting tool – Private Ralph Baggett, at left, had seven brothers who also served in the Corps. (NARA)

tactical flexibility, individual initiative, and active leadership at the lowest levels. The historical roles of landing parties operating far from headquarters, and small-unit patrols in the various counterinsurgency wars, both emphasized individual, on-the-spot leadership. Individual initiative and leadership were also necessary to deal with the considerable potential for chaos and the inevitable loss of key leaders in an amphibious assault. In the savage battle for Tarawa in 1943 the landing force was thrown into disarray by unexpected tides, savage Japanese resistance, and extremely high casualties. The landing forces literally rebuilt a combat organization in the midst of battle. Junior officers, non-commissioned officers, and even privates took command of groups of survivors, often from several different units, to organize small units and push inland.

To develop individual Marines as the basic units of an elite force, training was at once the harshest and most thorough provided by any branch of the American military. For enlisted recruits, or "boots" in Marine terminology, ten weeks of boot camp at Parris Island, South Carolina or San Diego, California, distilled away civilian attitudes, and hardened the recruit both physically and mentally. The boot learned such typical military skills as close-order drill, interior guard, rifle marksmanship, first aid and hygiene, fighting with knives and bayonets, and nuclear-chemical-biological warfare. As a naval service, they also learned swimming and water survival, and naval terminology and customs,

At the end of boot camp each new Marine learned his Military Occupational Specialty (MOS), the job he would do in the Corps. Regardless of MOS, the new Marines went on to Infantry Training Regiment (ITR), an even more grueling round-the-clock regimen of patrolling, small-unit tactics, escape and evasion, and urban combat, designed to teach them what infantry

combat was really like. The Marines learned to fire and to perform basic maintenance on virtually every infantry weapon in the inventory, from machine guns and grenades to rocket launchers.

After ITR, infantrymen attended the second session of ITR, more intensive training with particular assigned weapons such as machine guns and mortars. Marines in support units, from tanks and artillery to supply and clerical or aircraft maintenance, attended specialist schools conducted by the Marine Corps, Army, or Navy. Even after attendance at such schools, constant training took place within active units, and annual tests of physical fitness, academic subjects, and rifle marksmanship were mandatory. Officers attended a similarly rigorous Officers Basic School at Quantico, Virginia, followed by specialist training.[3]

Aside from the sheer intensity, if one aspect of training and indoctrination could be said to distinguish Marine training from that of the sister services, it might be History and Traditions. The subject was, not coincidentally, the very first chapter in *Handbook for Marines*, the boots' fundamental reference. The Marines emphasized physical fitness, but when called upon to perform feats that are seemingly beyond human ability or endurance, the will is often more important than the body. From his very first day of training, the boot learned stories of Marine heroism, endurance, and military achievement that would provide role models in his own time of trial. This pride of unit, along with personal pride at having endured the rigors of boot camp, and the determination not to fail in front of comrades, were the basis of the *esprit de corps* that drove units and individual Marines to excel in combat. If you sincerely believe that you are the best, often you will be.

The curriculum of the Infantry Training Regiment was even more intense than boot camp, operating around the clock. These new Marines of the 1st ITR at Camp Lejeune, North Carolina are negotiating barbed-wire obstacles under live machine gun fire. Explosive charges buried in the sandbagged pits rained dirt on the trainees and added to the noise and confusion. (NARA)

---

3 The training of Marines in this era is described more fully in *US Marine in Vietnam, 1965–73* (Osprey Warrior 23), and *US Marine Corps Tanker, 1965–70: Vietnam* (Osprey Warrior 90).

Unit organization

Since the early days of World War II and the rapid expansion of the Fleet Marine Force (FMF), the division has been the Corps' fundamental organizational unit. The division was originally conceived as a large "stand alone" formation capable of undertaking virtually any combat task in isolation, at considerable distance from its bases. Prior to 1941 the Marine Corps had fielded no unit larger than a brigade, and the divisions were raised as a series of all-arms brigades that included an infantry regiment, an artillery battalion, and a tank company. These brigades were later grouped as divisions, with the artillery battalions concentrated into an artillery regiment and the tank companies as a tank battalion. This early structure was important to the Corps' traditions, and individual Marines still trace their "lineage" by their regiment – for example, 5th Marines (infantry) or 14th Marines (artillery).

In the post-1945 reorganizations of the American military establishment, the Defense Unification Act prescribed the present strength of the Corps as at least four divisions. These are the 1st Marine Division, based in southern California; 2nd Marine Division, based in North Carolina; 3rd Marine Division, forward based in Okinawa and Hawaii; and the 4th Marine Division (Reserve) with component units based around the United States. Certain regiments were assigned to each of the four divisions. Most were the original units of the division from its inception in early World War II, while others had distinguished themselves in the Pacific fighting. One – the 4th Marines – was selected for purely sentimental reasons; it was the old "China Marines" brigade that served in northern China, surrendered on Corregidor, was reconstituted in part from the veterans of the disbanded Raider battalions, and fought on Guam as part of the Provisional Marine Brigade and on Okinawa as part of the 6th Marine Division.

The FMF Organization and Composition Board (known as the Hogaboom Board, after its chairman) of 1956 recommended that Marine divisions be reorganized to emphasize lightness and air transportability, with heavy

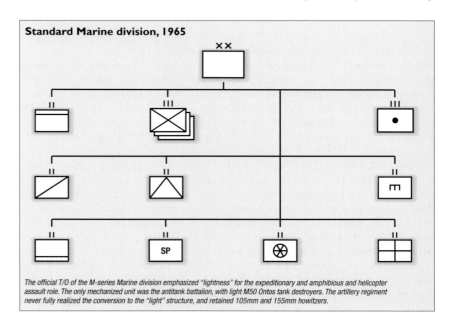

Standard Marine division, 1965

The official T/O of the M-series Marine division emphasized "lightness" for the expeditionary and amphibious and helicopter assault role. The only mechanized unit was the antitank battalion, with light M50 Ontos tank destroyers. The artillery regiment never fully realized the conversion to the "light" structure, and retained 105mm and 155mm howitzers.

equipment transferred to corps level. These corps-level assets were called Force Troops, and included most mechanized units such as the amphibian tractor and tank battalions, armored amphibian companies, and some artillery assets. Howtar wheeled mortars replaced some of the division's artillery. The only "heavy" or "armored" unit in the division was the Antitank Battalion, equipped with Ontos tank destroyers. The divisions were never completely restructured along the Hogaboom Board's suggested lines, and retained the 105mm and 155mm howitzers of the artillery regiment.

III Marine Amphibious Force

As the Marine coordinating command in Vietnam, this organization grew rapidly from the initially authorized division plus air wing structure. The peak strength was achieved in 1969, when it was a reinforced corps controlling two reinforced divisions, an air wing, combat elements directly under III MAF control, and the division-sized Force Logistics Command. With the reduction in forces III MAF was reduced in scale, until officially withdrawn in April 1971.

Marine divisions in Vietnam

In 1965 through 1967 Marine divisions followed the "light division" structure as the standard. This structure included a service battalion logistical and support element, and the antitank battalion was the division's only mechanized firepower. Tank battalions, heavy artillery, amphibian tractors, and force reconnaissance companies were all Force Troops units. Elements of these specialist units supported the division, but were not part of its fundamental structure.

When originally deployed, the divisions that served in Vietnam were the 1st (the oldest) and the 3rd Marine divisions. Their fundamental maneuver units were the 1st, 5th, 7th Marines (infantry) and 11th Marines (artillery), and the 3rd, 4th, 9th Marines (infantry) and 12th Marines (artillery) respectively.

III MAF organization peak strength, 1969

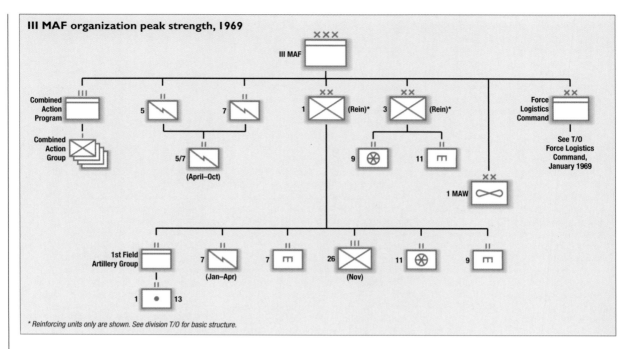

* Reinforcing units only are shown. See division T/O for basic structure.

Force Logistics Command, January 1969, HQ Danang

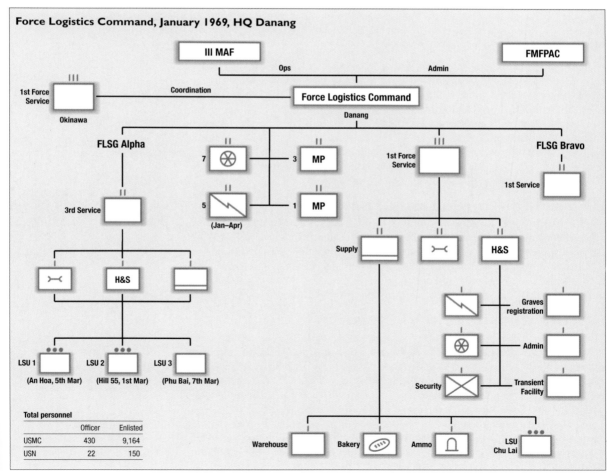

Total personnel		
	Officer	Enlisted
USMC	430	9,164
USN	22	150

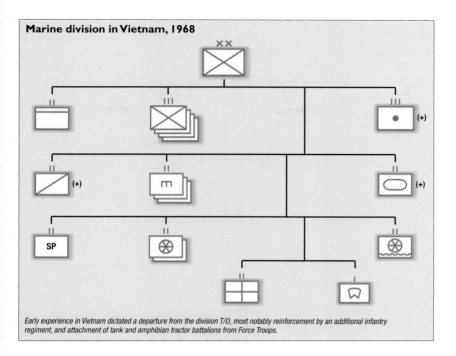

Marine division in Vietnam, 1968

Early experience in Vietnam dictated a departure from the division T/O, most notably reinforcement by an additional infantry regiment, and attachment of tank and amphibian tractor battalions from Force Troops.

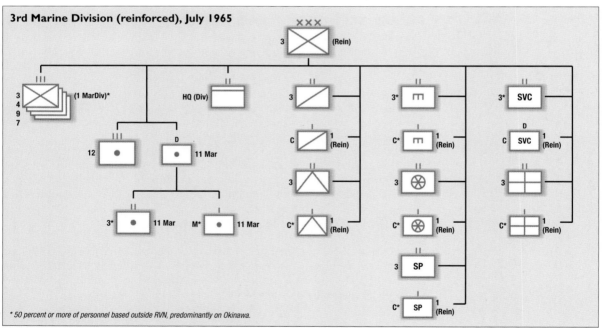

3rd Marine Division (reinforced), July 1965

* 50 percent or more of personnel based outside RVN, predominantly on Okinawa.

The exigencies of the war led to specific changes in the organizational structure at all levels, and none of the major units in Vietnam followed the "official" T/O or T/E. Changes effected in summer 1967 included the expansion of the division to four infantry regiments, reinforcement of the artillery regiment, and addition of more combat engineers. The reactivated 26th and 27th Marines and supporting units – 1st and 2nd battalions, 13th Marines (artillery), Alpha Company of the 5th Antitank Battalion, and elements of the 5th Tank Battalion – were deployed to Vietnam. The infantry regiments served as the extra infantry regiments of the "restructured" divisions for only brief periods (August 1966 until March 1970 for the 26th Marines, and February through September 1968 for the 27th Marines). The 13th Marines units subordinated to 1st Field Artillery Group, an interim organization under 1st Marine Division formed in 1968 and eliminated in July 1969. The single antitank company served as part of the 27th Marines, and the extra tanks were organizationally incorporated into the two divisional tank battalions.

Additional Motor Transport units were added to the restructured divisions, but the service battalions were removed from the division structure, and logistics functions concentrated in FLC. Some Force Troops units were permanently attached to the division, including a tank battalion, an amphibian tractor battalion, and a force reconnaissance company. In 1967 the division antitank battalion was reduced to a single small antitank company as part of the tank battalion. Medical support functions were also concentrated outside the division, with the medical battalion reduced to a small medical company and a dental company.

The inception of the divisions as brigades, though few Marines in Vietnam realized it, was still fundamental to the way the division functioned. The Direct Support Artillery battalions and the companies of the tank battalion were usually assigned to support one of the infantry regiments on a continuing basis, so that the men became "my" infantry or "my" gunners. This practice was not so systematic as in World War II and Korea, and tended to break down as units were "task organized" for specific operations. Under these circumstances the *esprit de corps* of Marines, and the common experience of boot camp and ITR, served to cement the broader relationship.

Unit strengths and tasks

Status of Forces reports, compiled weekly, indicate that virtually all units with the exception of infantry, where the heaviest casualties occurred, were maintained at or near authorized strength. However, not all personnel were "in country" simultaneously. Personnel (and sometimes equipment) might be distributed among various bases in Vietnam, home bases in Okinawa, Hawaii, or Japan, afloat with the Special Landing Forces, or on detached duty in the Philippines. In addition, some percentage was always on rest and recreation (R&R) leave in such places as Hong Kong, Bangkok, or even Hawaii.

It is impossible to assign specific strengths to units that were "task organized" because their personnel strength and equipment varied constantly with the assignment at hand. In most cases a range of reported strengths is provided.

In some cases entire units might be moved in and out of the country on a short-term basis. This was particularly true for some units like combat intelligence teams, specialized communications units, and medical or dental service units.

Another drain on manpower was area security. In addition to field operations, units were assigned variously sized zones around their base camps to patrol and suppress VC activity. Non-infantry units organized provisional rifle platoons for these security functions and as reaction forces.

Direct support, task forces, and unit cross-assignment

Under the Marine divisional structure, certain units such as artillery were in direct support of specific infantry regiments. Direct support meant that although command and support functions were still vested in the artillery regiment headquarters, the artillery battalion was in effect a dedicated asset under the immediate tactical control of the rifle regiment commander. The fourth battalion, equipped with powerful 155mm howitzers, was a general support battalion; its fires were controlled at division level although it might be temporarily placed in direct support for specific operations.

Combat demolition

In the Pacific War the Japanese were tenacious defenders of caves and bunker complexes, and "corkscrew and blowtorch" – demolition and flamethrower – tactics became a fundamental element of Marine tactics. By 1945 both weapons had ceased to be tools for specialists, becoming basic infantry weapons. In Vietnam combat demolitions were a primary task of combat engineers, but all infantry received basic training in assault demolitions.

Combat engineers had a wide variety of prepared explosive charges available, including shaped-charge cratering munitions and specialized explosives. Electrical detonation was still considered an engineer specialist task.

The basic demolition weapon was the M-37 demolition kit, a canvas bag with shoulder strap. Inside were two smaller bags, each with four 2½ lb. (c.1.3kg) blocks of white C4 plastic explosive; also included were two M15 priming assemblies, lengths of detonating cord with an attached booster charge. Satchel charges were normally prepared by crimping a blasting cap onto the end of a cut length of M700 safety fuze, green plastic tubing filled with powder that burned at 40 seconds per foot (30cm). Special crimping tools were provided, and this was the most dangerous part of the task. The cap was inserted into the explosive, and an M2 weatherproof fuze lighter (a 4in./10cm metal and paper tube with a pull ring) attached to the other end of the fuze cord. The user pulled the ring to ignite the fuze, then placed or hurled the charge against the target.

The M15 priming assemblies were used when the charges needed to be physically separated, but to detonate nearly simultaneously, as when cutting the support structures of a bridge. "Det cord" was a tube of PETN explosive inside a white, yellow, or yellow-and-white cloth covering, also available in 100 and 500ft (30m and 152m) rolls. Ignited by blasting caps, it detonated at 21,000 ft/sec (6,400m/sec). It could be used to detonate separated charges, and was commonly used by itself to cut trees or barriers.

The photo shows an engineer from A Company, 1st Engineer Battalion preparing to blow an enemy bunker during Operation *Meade River*. (MCRC)

In contrast to direct support, units might be "attached" to (i.e. placed under the administration and direct command of) another unit. This was the case for Force Troops units such as amphibian tractors, armored amphibians, tanks, and heavy artillery, which were attached to individual divisions in Vietnam but not officially part of their permanent structure. In turn the individual elements of these supporting combat arms, particularly tanks and amphibian tractors, were typically placed in direct support of subordinate units within the division for specific operations or periods. For the tanks in particular this meant that they might be tactically subordinated to infantry units for protracted periods.

For operational flexibility Marine Corps units in Vietnam adopted a "task force" organizational system, under which battalion-sized infantry units might be placed under the operational control of another formation, but not permanently transferred. In practice this meant that sometimes an infantry regiment headquarters might have all its subordinate battalions out "on loan." The controlling formation might be another regimental/brigade headquarters, or even an *ad hoc* headquarters established for some particular task.

An example of the latter was Task Force X-RAY during the fighting in Hue. X-RAY was the advance element of the 1st Division headquarters, intended to serve temporarily while the division shifted its tactical area of responsibility (TAOR). Instead, it was forced to assume overall command of the fighting in the city when the enemy's Tet Offensive erupted. It controlled a grab bag of available units that were either caught in transit or hastily dispatched from base areas. X-RAY directed: HQ Company, 1st Marines; 1st Battalion, 1st Marines; HQ Company, 5th Marines; 1st and 2nd battalions, and L Company of the 3rd Battalion, 5th Marines; 1st and 2nd battalions, 11th Marines (105mm howitzer); Provisional Platoon, 3rd Tank Battalion; Alpha and

The 81mm mortar was one of the infantry battalion's most potent weapons. This mortar belonging to a unit of the 26th Marines on Operation *Bold Mariner* is set up for all-around fire. The gunner is aligning the sight on the striped aiming stakes, visible at right. (MCRC)

Antitank companies, 1st Tank Battalion; 1st Engineer Battalion; 1st and 3rd Motor Transport battalions; 1st Shore Party Battalion; 7th Communications Battalion; 1st MP Company; Combat Intelligence Team, HQ Battalion, 1st Division; the first platoons of both 3rd and 34th Bridge companies (III MAF and Army); 1st Force Advisory Team; Hue Ramp Detachment, US Navy; MCB-8 and MCB-21, US Navy; Delta Battery, 1st Battalion, 44th Artillery (40mm SP AAA guns), US Army; and the 97th and 329th Transport companies (Heavy Boat), US Army.

Such task forces came and went with considerable alacrity, and their structure might change literally within days. Tracing which units were assigned to any particular short-lived task force is beyond the scope of this study.

The infantry regiment

The three or four infantry regiments were the striking power of the division, and the basic combat unit of the division. The brief addition of a fourth infantry regiment was an organizational anomaly, as the Marine Corps utilizes a "triangular" structure at most organizational levels. The rifle regiment consisted of three numbered maneuver battalions (1st through 3rd), controlled by a Headquarters and Services (H&S) company.

The regimental H&S company was primarily responsible for command, communications, and administrative functions of the regiment. While each Marine had his own assigned weapon, the company HQ included a small security platoon consisting of a staff sergeant and two nine-man squads. Each squad consisted of a squad leader and two four-man fire teams.

The regimental headquarters also controlled the Scout-Sniper platoon. It is important to realize that the Scout-Snipers were not simply long-range killers. As indicated by their name, the primary function of the two-man teams deployed by this platoon was intelligence gathering, either by stealthy observation or searching the bodies of their victims.

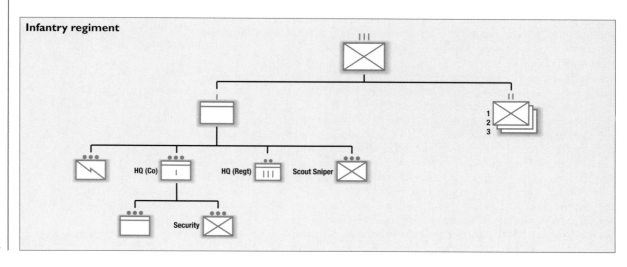

Infantry regiment

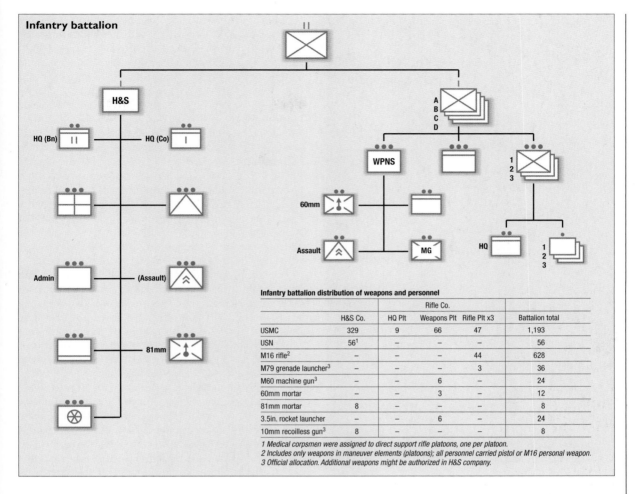

Infantry battalion

Infantry battalion distribution of weapons and personnel

		Rifle Co.			
	H&S Co.	HQ Plt	Weapons Plt	Rifle Plt x3	Battalion total
USMC	329	9	66	47	1,193
USN	56[1]	–	–	–	56
M16 rifle[2]	–	–	–	44	628
M79 grenade launcher[3]	–	–	–	3	36
M60 machine gun[3]	–	–	6	–	24
60mm mortar	–	–	3	–	12
81mm mortar	8	–	–	–	8
3.5in. rocket launcher	–	–	6	–	24
10mm recoilless gun[3]	8	–	–	–	8

1 Medical corpsmen were assigned to direct support rifle platoons, one per platoon.
2 Includes only weapons in maneuver elements (platoons); all personnel carried pistol or M16 personal weapon.
3 Official allocation. Additional weapons might be authorized in H&S company.

The infantry battalion

The infantry battalion was the basic tactical unit of the division, capable of independent and self-sufficient action, with the entire range of basic weapons for offensive or defensive operations. The "square" battalions were made up of an H&S company and four lettered companies. To minimize confusion, the 1st Battalion included Alpha, Bravo, Charlie and Delta companies; the 2nd Battalion Echo, Foxtrot, Golf and Hotel; and the 3rd Battalion India, Kilo, Lima and Mike. Juliet was not used. The mobility of the battalion and its component companies wa entirely by foot, with a minimal number of jeeps, trucks, and Mechanical Mules provided for administrative and some internal logistics functions. Trucks of the Motor Transport battalion, amphibian tractors, or helicopters provided tactical mobility as dictated by the current operation.

The battalion H&S Company provided command, medical, supply and administrative functions for the battalion. The H&S company also included antitank (106mm recoilless gun) and 81mm mortar platoons, the latter with its own fire direction control center and forward observers, and a small Assault section with 3½in. rocket launchers and two seldom-used M2 man-portable flamethrowers.

The infantry company

The infantry company was a small, self-contained combat unit with its own heavy weapons fire support. The nine-man Headquarters section with the company commander, company executive officer (who functioned as the fire-

This radiotelephone operator, or RTO, replaced the runners used to communicate in earlier conflicts. Note the staggering amount of equipment carried by this company commander's RTO, Mike Company, 3/7 on Operation *Citrus*. (MCRC)

support coordinator), first sergeant, supply sergeant, and supporting logistics, clerical, and communications personnel, controlled the Weapons platoon and three rifle platoons. Company commander was normally a captain's billet, but the rapid rotation of officers meant that the CO was often a senior lieutenant.

The rifle platoon's command section included a lieutenant platoon leader, a platoon sergeant (nominally a staff sergeant), and two or three private or PFC messengers. In Vietnam the latter were radiotelephone operators (RTO) with a man-portable PRC-25 radio, rather than message runners as envisaged in the original organization.

The three rifle squads of the platoon were the fundamental formation for Marine infantry tactics. Each squad consisted of three fire teams under a squad leader (nominally a sergeant, often a corporal), who exercised control through his fire-team leaders. As in the officer ranks, the effects of the rotation and replacement policy that limited tours of combat duty was such that this critical billet was often occupied by a very young NCO. It was a tribute to Marine training, discipline, and leadership practices that the system functioned as well as it did. In Vietnam an additional man designated a grenadier was added to the squad, armed with the M79 grenade launcher.

The fire team was a four-man maneuver element that could be reliably controlled by one man amid the confusion of combat. The primary task of the fire-team leader, nominally a corporal, was to direct and control his subordinates, and act as a link between them and the squad leader. His primary firepower was the automatic rifleman (nominally a lance corporal), whom he closely controlled. Two scout-riflemen (nominally privates or PFCs) acted as lead element, and supported and protected the automatic rifleman. This structure was designed around the older M14 rifle system, where most were semi-automatic rifles and one weapon in the team was equipped with a bipod and modified for full automatic fire. With the advent of the M16 system, the distinction was blurred by the fully automatic fire capability of any weapon.

The Weapons platoon controlled the heavy weapons, which could either be parceled out to other platoons or squads to augment their firepower in the

The M60 machine gun, affectionately known as "the pig" or "the black bitch," was the heavy firepower of the infantry company. Gun sections were grouped, or assigned to rifle squads depending upon the tactical situation. This section from Mike Company, 3/5 is in action near An Hoa. (MCRC)

assault, or grouped under central control. A small Headquarters section of the platoon leader, platoon sergeant, ammunition NCO, and two RTOs controlled the mortar, assault, and machine gun sections.

The NCO machine gun section leader supervised three machine gun squads, each with two machine gun teams of a gunner, assistant gunner (who carried the considerable load of maintenance equipment for the gun), and four ammunition carriers who carried belted ammunition and protected the gun team. This section was the company's heavy firepower.

The Assault section was intended for company antitank defense, and armed with the 3½in. rocket launcher. The NCO section leader supervised three rocket squads, each with two teams of gunner, assistant gunner, and an ammunition carrier. In practice, these weapons were used as direct fire "bunker busters" rather than in an antitank role.

The mortar section NCO supervised three 60mm mortar squads with one tube each, with a crew of five.

The artillery regiment

The artillery regiment consisted of a headquarters battery, and four numbered battalions. The 1st through 3rd battalions were direct support battalions, while the 4th Battalion was the general support battalion of heavier guns. The battalions of the regiment were self-transported, with sufficient trucks to act as prime movers for guns and personnel, to provide ammunition transport, and to transport the equipment of the battalion. Guns, including the heavy 155mm howitzers, could be airlifted by the Air Wing's heavy transport helicopters, giving the battalion the capability of occupying firebases in remote areas not accessible to vehicles. The 4.2in. mortars and Howtars of the mortar batteries were usually transported by the battery's own light trucks. They could be, though they seldom were, transported by men.

The regiment's headquarters battery provided command, administration, and logistical support for the firing battalions. The HQ battery coordinated the activities of the firing battalions, though the three direct support battalions were under immediate tactical control of their assigned rifle regiment. The 4th Battalion was held under regimental control, but could be assigned as direct support for specific operations. A senior officer and small staff were assigned to the division headquarters as liaison. In the artillery, medical services were distributed among the firing battalions, with only a small medical section to serve the needs of the regimental HQ battery.

Direct support battalions included a HQ battery and four firing batteries. The HQ battery provided fire direction control and general support, including

The 105mm howitzers of the direct support battalions were the workhorses of the artillery. This piece from Echo Battery, 2nd Battalion, 12th Marines at An Hoa is firing with a fraction of its normal crew. (MCRC)

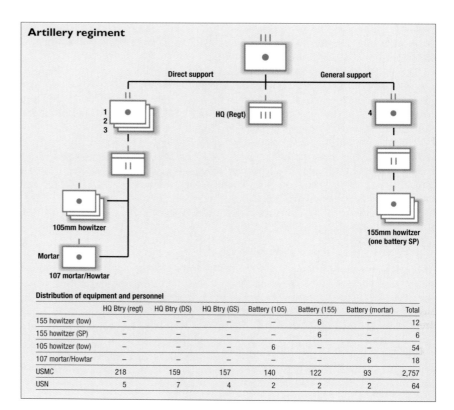

Artillery regiment

Direct support   General support

1 2 3   HQ (Regt)   4

105mm howitzer

Mortar

107 mortar/Howtar

155mm howitzer
(one battery SP)

The M109 self-propelled 155mm howitzer was scheduled to replace the towed guns in the general support battalion of the division artillery, but the costs of the war prevented the conversion. In Vietnam M109s equipped one battery of the battalion. (NARA)

Distribution of equipment and personnel

	HQ Btry (regt)	HQ Btry (DS)	HQ Btry (GS)	Battery (105)	Battery (155)	Battery (mortar)	Total
155 howitzer (tow)	–	–	–	–	6	–	12
155 howitzer (SP)	–	–	–	–	6	–	6
105 howitzer (tow)	–	–	–	6	–	–	54
107 mortar/Howtar	–	–	–	–	–	6	18
USMC	218	159	157	140	122	93	2,757
USN	5	7	4	2	2	2	64

five-ton 6x6 wrecker trucks and an M51 VTR in the maintenance section. The three 105mm howitzer batteries included six guns each, with prime movers, ammunition carriers, ambulances, repair vehicles, and general administrative transport. The standard truck of the 105mm batteries was the M35 2½ ton 6x6. The firing batteries were identified by letters: Alpha, Bravo, and Charlie in the 1st Battalion; Delta, Echo and Foxtrot in the 2nd Battalion; and Golf, Hotel and India in the 3rd Battalion. The fourth, or Mortar Battery, of the battalion was equipped with six guns, either M30 4.2in. bipod-mounted mortars or M98 Howtars as available. Artillery batteries almost always functioned as a single firing entity, but were internally subdivided into left and right platoons.

The 4th Battalion included an H&S Battery, and Kilo, Lima, and Mike batteries. Batteries were organized along parallel lines to the general support battalions, but equipped with towed 155mm howitzers and M54 five-ton 6x6 trucks. M109 SP howitzers were used in limited numbers, equipping one battery.

It is important to note that the structure of the artillery regiment was extremely flexible, and often deviated considerably from the official T/O, particularly during the drawdown period at the end of the war.

Smaller short-lived units included provisional batteries formed for special assignments, such as the 1st Provisional 155mm Howitzer Battery, 3rd Battalion 12th Marines at Khe Sanh in early 1968. Provisional batteries seem to have been primarily 155mm howitzer batteries, created to provide more firepower for specific operations.

Separate artillery batteries

Heavy Force Troops batteries in Vietnam included the 1st, 3rd and 7th 155mm Gun batteries, 1st and 3rd 8in. Howitzer batteries as parts of the 1st Field Artillery Group and subsequently attached to artillery regiments after the FAG was disbanded. These units were organized along the same lines as regular batteries, with six self-propelled guns, an M51 VTR for maintenance, and five-ton 6x6 trucks. The personnel strength was considerably higher than a typical battery – 238 Marines and five Navy medical corpsmen – to allow for separate maintenance and ammunition support functions, and larger gun crews.

Force Troops artillery units attached to III MAF included heavy guns like this 155mm M53 from the 7th 155mm Gun Battery. (MCRC)

The ANGLICO companies

Air-Naval Gunfire Liaison companies (ANGLICOs) were task organized, but typically included 110 Marines and 10 naval personnel. These units provided small – typically four- to six-man – detachments with specialized long-range communications equipment to control and coordinate gunfire from ships offshore, as well as Navy and Marine aircraft. ANGLICOs were considered communications units for strength reporting purposes.

The division reconnaissance battalion

The recon battalion was charged with reconnaissance and observation in direct support of the division's tactical activities. With virtually no organic transport except for a few administrative vehicles, it depended for mobility upon helicopters of the Air Wing. Individual platoons or companies operated in direct support of regimental operations, as assigned, where they provided not only patrolling services but also searches for booby-traps and concealed enemy arms caches.

The battalion was configured as a light infantry battalion, lacking the heavy weapons of the H&S company and infantry company weapons platoons, with a concomitant reduction in personnel. The battalion organization called for few heavy weapons, but like most units in Vietnam these units acquired and used large numbers of "unofficial" M60 machine guns. Similarly 81mm mortars were used in small numbers for base defense. The demands for reconnaissance became so great that the recon battalions grew to five line companies in 1968–69. In the mid-war period the force reconnaissance company assigned to support each division was also essentially absorbed as a sixth company within the recon battalion, until the October 1969 reorganization of the reconnaissance function.

The antitank battalion

The antitank battalion was an outgrowth of the experience in the Pacific War, when self-propelled antitank units were eventually grouped at division level. The battalion was equipped with the small M50A1 Ontos, originally designed for Army airborne forces. Tactically, platoons of tank destroyers were subordinated to infantry units for direct fire support, in the same fashion as tanks.

In December 1967 the antitank battalion was cadred (reduced in size) and placed as an additional reinforced company in the tank battalions.

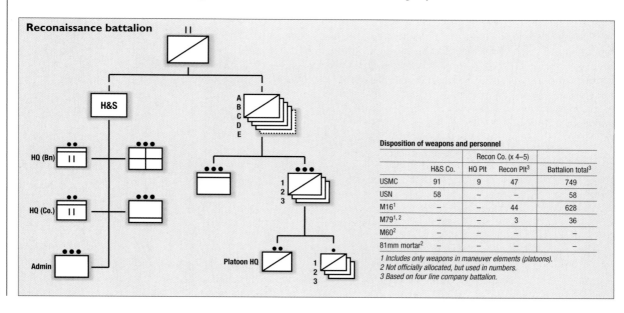

Reconaissance battalion

Disposition of weapons and personnel

	H&S Co.	Recon Co. (x 4–5)		Battalion total[3]
		HQ Plt	Recon Plt[3]	
USMC	91	9	47	749
USN	58	–	–	58
M16[1]	–	–	44	628
M79[1, 2]	–	–	3	36
M60[2]	–	–	–	–
81mm mortar[2]	–	–	–	–

1 Includes only weapons in maneuver elements (platoons).
2 Not officially allocated, but used in numbers.
3 Based on four line company battalion.

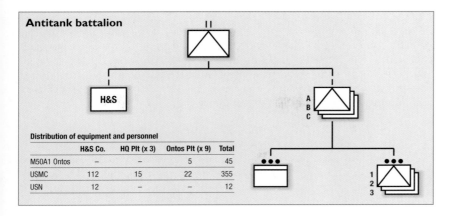

Antitank battalion

Distribution of equipment and personnel	H&S Co.	HQ Plt (x 3)	Ontos Plt (x 9)	Total
M50A1 Ontos	–	–	5	45
USMC	112	15	22	355
USN	12	–	–	12

The light M50 Ontos tank destroyer packed considerable firepower in its six 106mm recoilless guns (only four are fitted to this one), but its thin armor made it vulnerable even to small-arms fire at close ranges. (NARA)

The tank battalion

The tank battalion provided detachments of tanks that might serve either in direct support of infantry units, or be attached for prolonged periods. On the offensive, gun tanks were employed as direct fire artillery in support of infantry, and seldom used in formations larger than a five-tank platoon. Flame tanks were generally employed as single vehicles. Tanks were used extensively as convoy escorts, and the vast majority of tank losses, both destroyed and damaged, were to mines and road ambushes. Documents provided by Colonel Joe Sleger (USMC, ret.), commander of 3rd Tank Battalion, indicated an incidence of about 18 mine strikes per month.

In the defense, tanks were utilized singly or more commonly in heavy (three-tank) or light (two-tank) sections as bridge and firebase security. Battalion officers were not happy with their tanks serving as fixed defenses. Near tank unit encampments *ad hoc* platoons were typically on standby as a reaction force to help infantry repel assaults or to aid ambushed truck convoys. These armored reaction forces were themselves almost inevitably ambushed.

The tank battalions in Vietnam each consisted of an H&S company, and three lettered line companies (Alpha, Bravo, Charlie) equipped with M48A3 tanks. In December 1967 the division antitank battalions were eliminated from the divisions in Vietnam, and an antitank company was added to each tank battalion.

Tank battalion

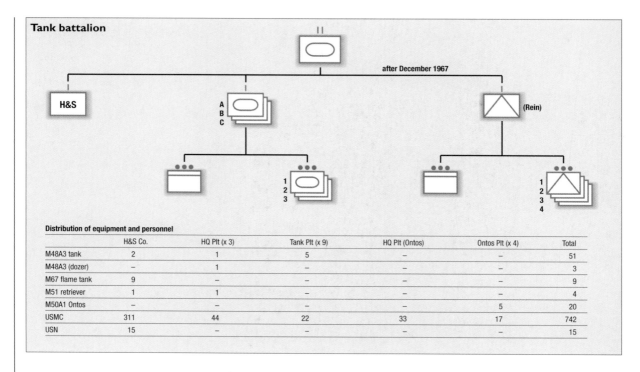

after December 1967

H&S

A
B
C

(Rein)

1
2
3

1
2
3
4

Distribution of equipment and personnel

	H&S Co.	HQ Plt (x 3)	Tank Plt (x 9)	HQ Plt (Ontos)	Ontos Plt (x 4)	Total
M48A3 tank	2	1	5	–	–	51
M48A3 (dozer)	–	1	–	–	–	3
M67 flame tank	9	–	–	–	–	9
M51 retriever	1	1	–	–	–	4
M50A1 Ontos	–	–	–	–	5	20
USMC	311	44	22	33	17	742
USN	15	–	–	–	–	15

The H&S company was responsible for command and administration, heavy maintenance, supply, motor transport, and medical support. The H&S company included a flame tank platoon with nine M67A2 flame tanks organized into three sections of three tanks each. The command section had two gun tanks for the commanding officer and executive officer. The maintenance section included one M51 tank recovery vehicle (VTR) based on the chassis of the M103A2 heavy tank, and three five-ton wrecker trucks.

The headquarters platoon of each tank company had two gun tanks (one equipped with an M8 bulldozer blade and the special hydraulics package necessary to operate it) and a single M51 VTR. The three numbered tank platoons each had five M48A3 tanks, which could be subdivided into a heavy section with three tanks under the platoon leader, and a two-tank light section under the senior NCO.

Even the most unlikely Marine units participated in Civic Action programs within their areas. This M48A3 dozer blade tank from 3rd Tank Battalion is clearing trees around a village; fires were a constant hazard during the dry season. (MCRC)

Very much a rarity in Marine service, the H&S Company of 3rd Tank Battalion had a handful of M113 personnel carriers that they used as mobile command post and combat logistics vehicles. (NARA)

The antitank company incorporated into the tank battalion was larger than the standard company, and personnel strengths varied. Four numbered antitank platoons of five Ontos each included an officer and 14 enlisted men. A small Headquarters Section with an officer, a medical corpsman, and eight or more enlisted men served the company. A small liaison section of an officer and six enlisted men were seconded to the battalion H&S company to provide support specific to the Ontos unit.

3rd Tank Battalion also included a section of three M113 personnel carriers used as a mobile command center and as logistics carriers.

Tank units did not serve the entire duration of the war. Elements of 3rd Tank Battalion arrived with the first ground units in July 1965, and the battalion departed in October 1969. The 1st Tank Battalion arrived in March 1966 and departed March 1970. Elements of the 5th Tank Battalion served briefly in 1968 as reinforcement for units in country, but official records do not include the 5th Tank as a unit in Vietnam.

The amphibian tractor battalion

Though vehicles were armed with light machine guns (and as the war went on, an increasing array of heavy weapons in improvised mounts), doctrinally this

The definitive Marine vehicle was the LVTP-5 amphibian tractor, often pressed into service as a personnel carrier despite its unsuitability for prolonged operation on land. Note the sandbag superstructure, and how the infantry are riding on top. (NARA)

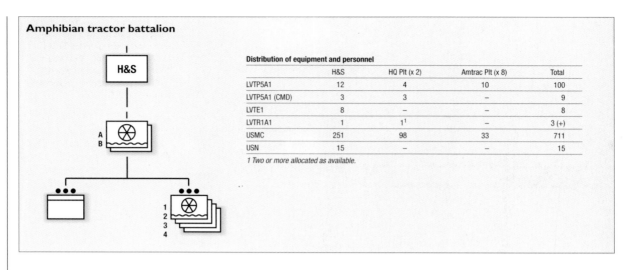

Amphibian tractor battalion

Distribution of equipment and personnel

	H&S	HQ Plt (x 2)	Amtrac Plt (x 8)	Total
LVTP5A1	12	4	10	100
LVTP5A1 (CMD)	3	3	–	9
LVTE1	8	–	–	8
LVTR1A1	1	1[1]	–	3 (+)
USMC	251	98	33	711
USN	15	–	–	15

1 Two or more allocated as available.

unit was considered to have a strictly tactical transport function, with no combat capability of its own. An amtrac company transported and supported an infantry battalion, with each platoon supporting an infantry company. Variable-sized detachments of amtracs were placed in direct support of infantry units for specific operations.

The H&S company provided administrative, command, communications, heavy repair, medical, and engineering functions. It included twelve LVTP5A1 personnel carriers that served as utility vehicles and a battalion reserve, three LVTP5A1 (CMD) variants, one LVTP1A1 recovery vehicle, and eight LVTE1 engineer vehicles.

The battalion included only two line companies (Alpha and Bravo), though the commandant might authorize a third company. Each company consisted of a headquarters section, equipped as shown in the unit diagram. The amtrac units suffered frequent mine strikes, and numerous breakdowns caused by prolonged land operation for which the vehicles were never designed. As a result, amtrac companies included two or three LVTRs, rather than the one authorized.

The amtrac battalions took advantage of the amphibious capabilities in the local security functions, using their amtracs to patrol rivers and coastal areas. In this they were supported by their own provisional rifle platoons, and reinforced by detachments from the 1st Armored Amphibian Company.

The armored amphibian company

The Marine Corps possessed large stocks of the last assault amphibians, or cannon-armed amtracs, but activated only the 1st Armored Amphibian Company. This company was equipped with eighteen LVTH6s, armed with a 105mm howitzer and doctrinally an artillery weapon. These were divided into three platoons, and supported by a headquarters platoon that provided minimal truck transport. Doctrinally the armored amphibians were artillery rather than tanks, but were generally parceled out in two- or three-vehicle sections for patrol support or direct fire support on specific operations in areas inaccessible to tanks.

The engineer battalions

The 1st and 3rd Engineer battalions were configured as divisional combat engineer units for support of the 1st and 3rd divisions, respectively. These units were tasked with light and heavy construction support of the division, building almost any conceivable facility including but not limited to bridges and culverts, airfields, fortified positions such as firebases, roads, and building complexes, and constructed and operated ferries. They also conducted combat

The most hazardous task for the division engineers was the daily sweep for mines planted in the roads each night by VC sappers. The general absence of paved roads made the enemy's task far simpler. (MCRC)

Engineer battalion

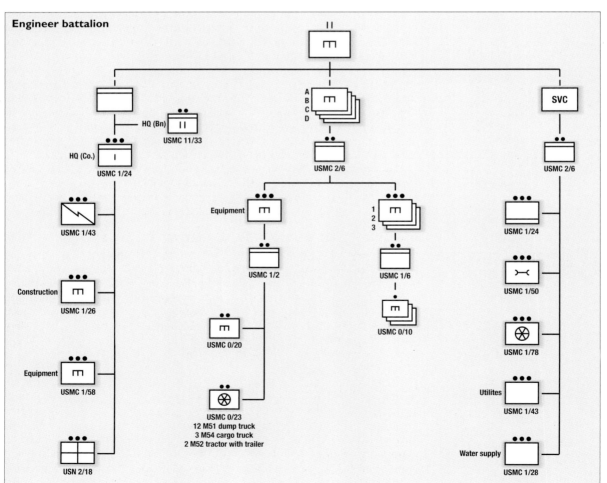

HQ (Bn) — USMC 11/33

HQ (Co.) — USMC 1/24

USMC 1/43

Construction — USMC 1/26

Equipment — USMC 1/58

USN 2/18

A B C D — USMC 2/6

Equipment — USMC 1/2

USMC 0/20

USMC 0/23
12 M51 dump truck
3 M54 cargo truck
2 M52 tractor with trailer

1 2 3 — USMC 1/6

USMC 0/10

SVC — USMC 2/6

USMC 1/24

USMC 1/50

USMC 1/78

Utilites — USMC 1/43

Water supply — USMC 1/28

35

demolitions, mine clearance operations, laid and lifted "friendly" minefields, and taught division schools in mine warfare, demolitions, and VC booby-traps.

Engineer units operated not only familiar construction machinery, but quarries and rock crushing plants, concrete and asphalt (macadam) plants, and sawmills. One of the most important tasks was operating centralized water supply points.

Engineer units were often task organized, which meant that they had no fixed structure but evolved with the role they filled. This is particularly the case with the 7th, 9th and 11th Engineer battalions.

Engineer battalions had a headquarters company, a service company, and four lettered engineer companies. The headquarters company provided administrative, communications, mess, and medical support. The large engineer equipment platoon operated and maintained specialized heavy equipment like large bulldozers, backhoes, cranes, pile drivers, large graders, and such oddities as 2½-ton spray trucks used to oil roads to reduce dust.

The service company provided supplementary transport including five-ton dump body trucks, supply, and equipment maintenance for the battalion. The utilities platoon helped operate and maintain fixed infrastructure like electrical systems and permanent water purification plants. One of the most important units was the water supply platoon. This platoon operated trailer-mounted water purification plants called Erdalators that could remove silt and suspended matter, filter, and purify even contaminated stream water. Producing from 1–3,000 gallons (about 4,000 to 12,000 liters) per day – the larger number was achieved using separate large rubberized settling tanks – one unit could adequately supply an infantry battalion under adverse conditions.

The engineer company headquarters provided minimal administrative functions. The equipment platoon's engineer equipment section provided maintenance and operators for three to five tracked or wheeled graders such as the MS200 wheeled grader and the small Case 500 bulldozer which could be disassembled for transport as two helicopter loads. The motor transport section supported the company's wheeled transport including twelve M51 dump body trucks, three M54 2½-ton 6x6 cargo trucks, and two M-54 tractor-trailer units for hauling heavy equipment.

Though organizations were standardized, the equipment of the engineer battalion fluctuated with the tasks assigned. The 9th Engineer Battalion operated this trailer-mounted rock-crushing plant as part of a road improvement program. (MCRC)

Road and bridge repair and improvement were a constant burden. Here a wheeled dozer from 9th Engineer Battalion works on a bridge approach. Note the water can and weapons close at hand. (MCRC)

The three numbered engineer platoons provided the combat and construction labor for the company. The 7th, 9th, and 11th Engineer battalions provided many of the same services to augment the division's engineer support.

All the engineer companies were assigned 15–20 mile (23–33km) sections of important supply roads to keep open, including removing wrecked vehicles and daily sweeps for mines.

Company A, 3rd Engineer Battalion and Company A, 5th Engineer Battalion reinforced the 1st Engineer Battalion. The 3rd Engineers were augmented by the 11th Engineer Battalion, which in turn was reinforced by the 3rd Bridge Company. The 7th Engineer Battalion, reinforced by the 1st Bridge Company, and the 9th Engineer Battalion, were attached to III MAF. The 9th Engineers were primarily responsible for road and bridge maintenance, projects connected to the CAP, and in 1969 also supported the Army's light Americal Division.

Marine engineers worked alongside and performed many of the same functions as the 5–12 Navy "Seabee" construction battalions assigned to Naval Support Facility, Danang. Four battalions of the US Army's 45th Engineer Group also supported activities of III MAF. One senior MAF officer remarked that with so many engineers stirring about, the lines of responsibility often became "blurred," and it was often impossible to determine which engineer formations were performing which tasks.

Engineers were armed with infantry weapons including rifles, pistols, M79 grenade launchers, light and heavy (generally truck-mounted) machine guns, and one to two 81mm mortars per battalion.

The vehicles of the heavy motor transport battalions made up most of the rough rider convoys that moved heavy cargo throughout the I Corps region. These trucks of the 7th Motor Transport Batallion are negotiating the Hai Phuong Pass. (MCRC)

The motor transport battalions

The 1st and 3rd Motor Transport (MT) battalions were configured as standard divisional "Motor T" battalions, tasked with providing basic logistical transport and limited tactical mobility to the infantry regiments. The battalion had an H&S company that provided administrative and heavy maintenance services for the battalion, including five-ton 6x6 wrecker trucks. The three lettered truck companies

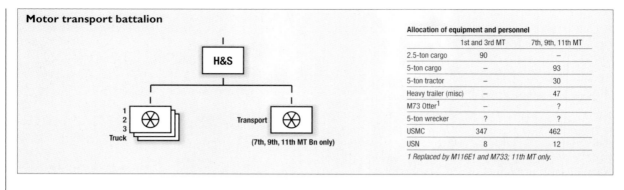

Motor transport battalion

H&S

1
2
3
Truck

Transport

(7th, 9th, 11th MT Bn only)

Allocation of equipment and personnel

	1st and 3rd MT	7th, 9th, 11th MT
2.5-ton cargo	90	–
5-ton cargo	–	93
5-ton tractor	–	30
Heavy trailer (misc)	–	47
M73 Otter[1]	–	?
5-ton wrecker	?	?
USMC	347	462
USN	8	12

1 Replaced by M116E1 and M733; 11th MT only.

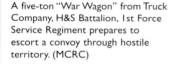

A five-ton "War Wagon" from Truck Company, H&S Battalion, 1st Force Service Regiment prepares to escort a convoy through hostile territory. (MCRC)

each contained thirty 2½-ton 6x6 trucks. The battalion's main tasks were to provide routine transport for the division.

For a brief period Company A (less one platoon), 5th MT Battalion reinforced the 1st MT Battalion, 1st Division. Similarly, a platoon from Company A, 5th MT Battalion reinforced the 3rd MT Battalion.

The 7th, 9th, and 11th MT battalions were task organized for heavy transport. The H&S company controlled four truck companies. Alpha, Bravo and Charlie companies each included 31 five-ton 6x6 trucks. The transport company included thirty 6x6 tractor units, with heavy trailers of various types including flatbed, van, and bulk fuel transporters. The 11th and 9th MT battalions were assigned to support the 1st and 3rd divisions, respectively. The 7th MT Battalion was assigned to FLC.

The 11th MT Battalion also operated a few M73 Otter tracked amphibious logistics carriers. The M116 Husky logistics carrier, and the M733 amphibious full-tracked assault vehicle, an open-topped armored version of the Husky, replaced the Otters but were never used in significant numbers.

Truck Company, H&S Battalion, 1st Force Service Regiment was an oversized company that provided specialized vehicles, as well as 2½- and 5-ton trucks. The large armored 5-ton gun trucks used for convoy escort were assigned from this company.

The shore party battalion

Shore Party battalions were transferred early on from division to III MAF control. These units had a loose structure, but were in effect task organized. Reported battalion strengths varied from 273 Marines and eight Navy medical personnel to 567 Marines and 19 Navy corpsmen, depending upon time period and responsibilities. The official T/O of the battalion called for an H&S company and three letter-designated companies, but in Vietnam a fourth company was added to support the additional infantry regiment.

Line companies acted as military cargo handlers, and managed all aerial and truck re-supply activities in forward combat areas.

The military police battalion

The typical function for a Marine Corps military police (MP) battalion was to provide beach traffic control, convoy escort and guidance, and to guard both criminal and enemy prisoners. In a counter-guerrilla war marked by the use of bombs and assassinations, the demand for MPs was significantly increased in order to provide security for base areas and locations within civilian communities where Marine facilities such as liaison or services functioned. The 1st and 3rd MP battalions provided security and traffic control within the I Corps region.

The battalion's H&S company provided the usual administrative, communications, medical, and supply functions for the battalion. The S-2/S-3 section managed counterintelligence information applicable to the unit's security work. The Sentry Dog Platoon provided security for fixed installations

The shore party battalion, the division's organic logistics unit, was responsible not only for moving supplies but related activities as well. These Marines from 3rd Shore Party Battalion are building a boat ramp at Quang Tri. (MCRC)

Marines of the 1st Shore Party Battalion unload ammunition and vehicles at the Hue Navy Boat Ramp during the fighting in early 1968. Note the gas masks, worn because of tear gas drifting across the river from fighting in the Imperial City. (MCRC)

The primary tasks of the MP companies were to control the flow of military traffic, and to provide security for support units. Here MPs of the 3rd MP Battalion and their Vietnamese counterparts control the admittance of local civilian employees in Danang. (MCRC)

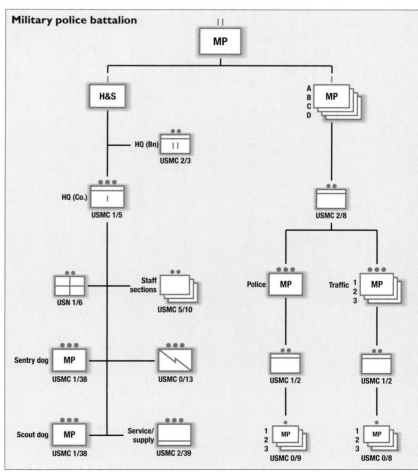

Military police battalion

MP battalions also provided security and scout dog services, like this scout dog team supporting the 5th Marines near An Hoa. Scout dogs were so highly valued that wounded dogs sometimes received medical evacuation priority over wounded Marines. (MCRC)

and base areas, with dogs trained to attack and hold intruders. The Scout Dog Platoon provided services to combat units in the field using dogs trained to alert to the scent of an enemy, detecting ambushes and hidden fugitives.

The battalion's four companies (Alpha through Delta) were each subdivided into a small headquarters, an MP platoon for investigation of criminal activities, and three traffic platoons that also provided security functions. Personnel were equipped with side arms, rifles, shotguns, and light machine guns.

The force reconnaissance company

Force recon companies in Vietnam were in effect task organized as very small rifle companies but with considerably heavier firepower. Doctrinally, force recon was an outgrowth of the Amphibious Corps recon companies of World War II, and was intended to provide beach reconnaissance in advance of landings and long-range patrolling during land campaigns.

In Vietnam force recon operated in the strategic and deep tactical information and target acquisition role in operational support of divisions as well as III MAF. Initially under III MAF control, by 1969 these units had gradually been absorbed into the division recon battalions of the divisions they supported (1st Force Recon Company for 1st Marine Division, 3rd Force Recon for the 3rd Marine Division). By late 1969, III MAF felt that the long-range patrolling elements of MACV, the Special Operations Group, was no longer meeting III MAF's requirements for timely and relevant information gathering. In October the force recon companies were returned to direct control of III MAF, under the newly created Surveillance and Reconnaissance Center.

The typical mission for force recon was the "Sting Ray," in which teams of five to ten men were inserted to observe and summon artillery and air attacks. If they became engaged, they could either be extracted, or reinforced by an on-call reaction force if the tactical situation seemed suitable to inflict casualties on NVA forces.

The typical strength for a full strength force recon company was 145 to 156 Marines, supported by seven Navy corpsmen.

The Combined Action Force

The small units that constituted the bulk of the CAP were intended to be as self-sufficient as possible, and the program did not have the logistical or administrative "tail" of most units. The higher-level commands of the Combined Action Force were primarily to handle personnel administration. The organization was highly variable because the strengths of headquarters or command levels varied with the number of field personnel assigned to the program. The Force consisted of a minimal administrative headquarters under III MAF, which at times controlled up to four groups, also minimal and with no set size or organization. A group controlled four to twelve letter-designated companies, and the bulk of manpower was at company level. Company personnel were drawn from and supported by the local division, and were not carried on the CAP manpower reports.

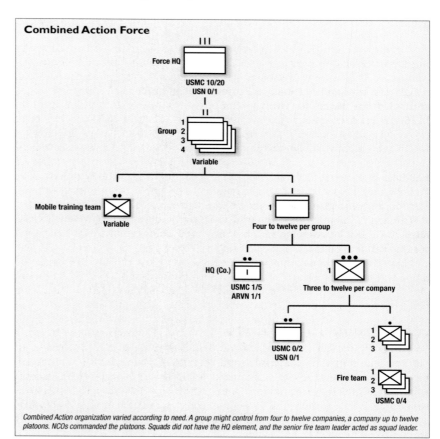

Combined Action organization varied according to need. A group might control from four to twelve companies, a company up to twelve platoons. NCOs commanded the platoons. Squads did not have the HQ element, and the senior fire team leader acted as squad leader.

The Combined Action Company (CACO) consisted of a small company headquarters of one officer and five enlisted men who handled communications and basic administrative duties; this element also included one ARVN officer and one enlisted man as liaison and interpreters. A company might control from three to twelve Combined Action platoons. A platoon headquarters consisted of two enlisted men, one a senior NCO. A supporting Navy medical corpsman monitored the health of the Marines, and treated civilians as he traveled about the countryside. Each of the three twelve-man squads consisted of only the four-man fire teams; the senior fire team leader functioned as the squad leader. The platoons worked with local Regional Forces and Popular Forces militias, which usually had about 40 combatants to a platoon, but strengths of these indigenous units were highly variable.

The small CAP units typically were equipped with weapons above what was rated for a unit of comparable size. Platoons commonly included M79s, less commonly M60 machine guns, and one 81mm mortar.

There was no logistical or support structure organic to the CAP. Necessary rations and clothing, ammunition, high-level ordnance repair, medical services and any other support were provided through the division in whose TAOR the platoon operated.

Health services units

The US Navy provided all medical and dental services. While the number of physicians and medical corpsmen organic to combat units was usually fixed, higher-echelon units were task organized. Medical battalions provided surgical and emergency services to combat units. The 1st and 3rd Medical battalions varied in strength from 163 Marines and 276 Navy personnel, to 203 Marines and 346 Navy personnel. The 1st Hospital Company at Danang had 56 Marines and 68 naval personnel.

A fire team from Combined Action Platoon 2-5-3 (2nd Group, 5th Company, 3rd Platoon), Hoa Da Village answers mail call. The "Care Package" included American newspapers, canned goods like vegetables, and books. These small teams were often heavily armed – note the M79 visible behind the man second from right. (NARA)

The 1st, 3rd, 11th and 13th Dental companies varied from a minimum of 30 to a maximum of 83 naval personnel, with from zero to 52 Marines attached.

Miscellaneous units

Other units that served as part of III MAF included communications and radio battalions, the 1st Searchlight Battery, 1st and 3rd Bridge companies, and the 7th Bulk Fuel Company.

Communications battalions and radio battalions operated long-range communications, fixed radio installations, and permanent telephone and teletype facilities including communications with commands outside Vietnam. These units were task organized, and varied from a minimum strength of 364 Marines (1st Radio Bn, 1969) up to 1,060 Marines and 13 Navy personnel (9th Communications Bn, 1969).

The bridge companies were task organized, with strengths of 89 to 102 Marines. The 7th Bulk Fuel Company operated fuel depots, and was task organized but with a typical strength of 160 Marines.

Intelligence Translation Teams and Combat Intelligence Teams were small (generally eight to fifteen-man) teams assigned to III MAF. These units moved in and out of country, depending upon need.

Logistics

It is an old military axiom that amateurs argue tactics, while professionals discuss logistics. The ability of the Marines to sustain themselves as a self-sufficient force was the major factor in the decision to first commit Marines rather than Army troops. The irony was that logistical expertise had long been one of the Corps' weaknesses, in execution if not in theory.

The Corps had traditionally operated its own procurement system that supplied uniforms and equipment specific to the Corps, but with a history of serving as small landing forces, the Corps generally dealt with operational logistics by local improvisation. Nowhere was this more obvious than with the misadventures of Col Joseph H. Pendleton's 4th Marines in the first intervention in the Dominican Republic.

In April 1916 that unhappy country teetered on the brink of civil war. Pendleton's expeditionary force landed at ports along the north coast, and reinforced by ship's guard detachments and infantry companies from the Haiti occupation force, marched in two columns against rebel strongholds in the Cibao Valley.

Pendleton's victory over the ill-armed and poorly organized rebel forces was a foregone conclusion. The expeditionary force had no supplies to maintain them in action other than the rations and ammunition that they carried with them or could be supplied by naval vessels, and they were forced to rely entirely upon local transport. The march of 70 miles (116km) would hardly have constituted a major achievement by any European army, but for the inadequately equipped Marines, it was an ordeal. In the words of historian Robert Millett, "The only imponderables were the degree of rebel resistance and the efficiency of the Marines' jury-rigged supply train of primitive trucks, wagons, mule trains, and ox-carts."

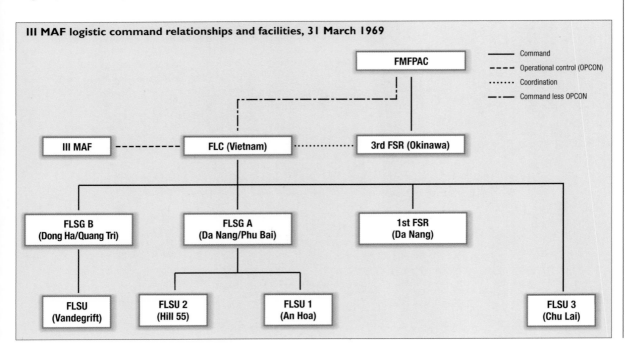

III MAF logistic command relationships and facilities, 31 March 1969

In World War I the Marines' basic requirements were met by the American and French Army supply systems. Only when the Marines began to ponder the causes of the Gallipoli failure did operational logistics emerge as a key planning issue. The Marines introduced combat loading of transports (loading ships in such a way that items likely to be needed first are on top of the cargo in the ship's hold, with items needed later stored in the depths), and amphibian tractors as ship-to-shore logistics carriers. However, they remained wedded to handling bulk cargo by huge teams of military stevedores – the Shore Party. This system came close to causing disaster at both Guadalcanal and Tarawa.

The Marines profited from Army innovations like palletized cargo and the DUKW amphibian truck. Their own innovations included barge-mounted cranes for unloading boats at the shore, floating "barrel corrals" for managing masses of fuel, and systems for dispatching critical cargo directly from the ship to the front lines without intermediary handling. By the Okinawa campaign, and despite critical shortages of cargo trucks and heavy equipment, two Marine divisions and their supporting elements achieved the unloading of over 800,000 measured tons of supplies and equipment from 458 ships. In the Korean conflict the relatively small Marine force of a single division and air elements was supported largely by Eighth Army logistics, with specialist support by the divisions' own logistical elements.

Throughout World War II and Korea the Marine Corps utilized a "push logistics" concept, in which logistical planning was driven from the rear. Operational planners used prior operations to predict a constantly shifting baseline of assumed requirements for everything from ammunition to grave markers. This concept was exemplified by the concept of a "unit of fire," the presumed quantity of all types of ammunition that would be expended by a unit in a "typical" day of combat. Forced upon planners by a combination of slow communications, even slower processing of requests in a paper-based bureaucracy, and slow loading and movement of surface shipping, this system naturally led to intermittent shortages of some items and a surfeit of others in the front lines.

The buildup

In Vietnam, III MAF would have to maintain two Marine divisions and their complementary air wing, and all supporting elements like additional engineer units. The requirements for the supply and repair of uniquely Marine Corps items from uniforms to amphibian tractors and different helicopters meant that such support could not be readily met by the Army structure supporting MACV.

In fact, the amount of support to be provided by MACV was contentious from the start. The first landing force, the 9th MEB, carried 15 days' rations, and there was a dispute whether MACV or 7th Fleet would supply immediate

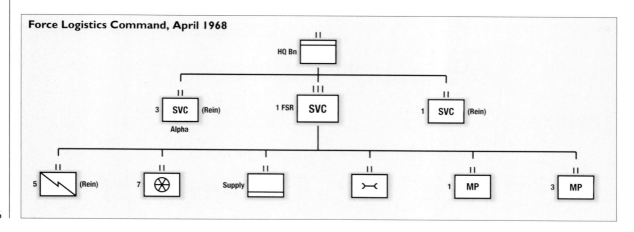

Force Logistics Command, April 1968

Early computers, operated by data processing platoons of Force Logistics Command, made the "pull" logistical system possible. Air-conditioned facilities required for the IBM360 computers made this a cushy assignment indeed. (MCRC)

stocks. Eventually Westmoreland approved the provision of some support at the end of March 1965.

Arrival of Marine logistical units from the 3rd Service Battalion and Force Service Regiment (FSR) on 22 March provided III MAF with their own support. The locations of the main supporting facilities were established at this time, with Force Logistics Support (FLS) Unit-1 at Chu-Lai and FLS Unit-2 at Phu Bai. Both units were part of the Force Support Logistics Group.

During this early buildup, the logistics groups were overburdened by the necessity to fulfill both their own tasks and the duties of operating port facilities normally handled by the Navy. During this period the III MAF was

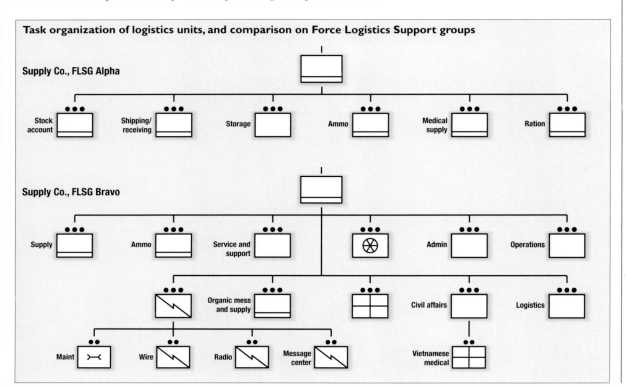

Task organization of logistics units, and comparison on Force Logistics Support groups

Force Logistics Command, HQ Danang, April 1970

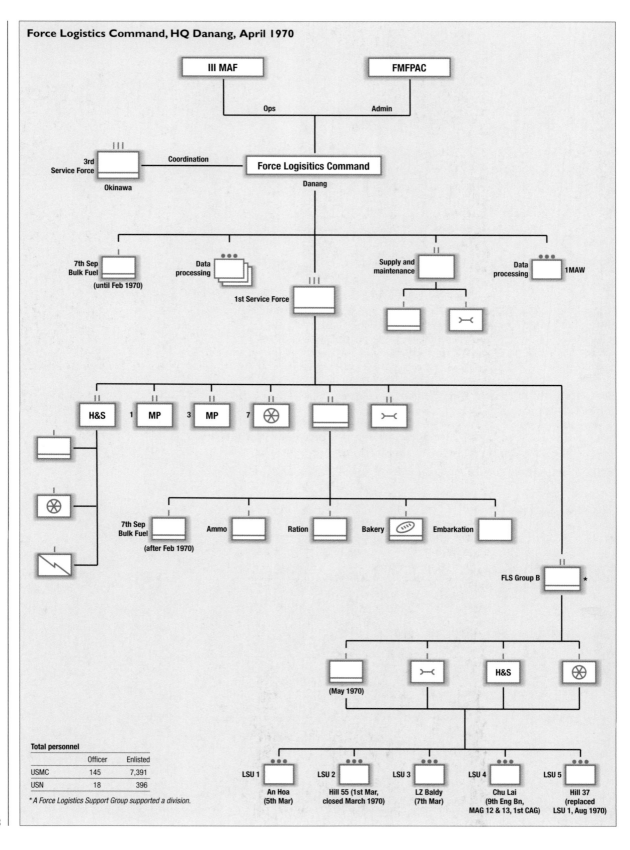

| III MAF | | FMFPAC |

Ops — Admin

3rd Service Force (Okinawa) — Coordination — **Force Logisitics Command** (Danang)

7th Sep Bulk Fuel (until Feb 1970)

Data processing

1st Service Force

Supply and maintenance

Data processing — 1MAW

H&S

1 MP

3 MP

7

7th Sep Bulk Fuel (after Feb 1970)

Ammo

Ration

Bakery

Embarkation

FLS Group B *

(May 1970)

H&S

LSU 1	LSU 2	LSU 3	LSU 4	LSU 5
An Hoa (5th Mar)	Hill 55 (1st Mar, closed March 1970)	LZ Baldy (7th Mar)	Chu Lai (9th Eng Bn, MAG 12 & 13, 1st CAG)	Hill 37 (replaced LSU 1, Aug 1970)

Total personnel

	Officer	Enlisted
USMC	145	7,391
USN	18	396

A Force Logistics Support Group supported a division.

48

responsible for all support and construction activities. Shortages of heavy equipment and the burden of airfield construction meant that other improvements such as bases and even hospitals were delayed. Road maintenance in particular suffered, since the Vietnamese system was never intended to support heavy military vehicles, and the monsoon was fast approaching. In late August the 7th Engineer Battalion, a Force Troops heavy construction unit, was attached to III MAF, followed by the 30th Naval Construction Battalion and civilian contractors.

In mid-October 1965 the Navy established Naval Support Activity at Danang, relieving III MAF of some of its more burdensome support activities. At its peak, this organization employed over 11,000 naval personnel, 6,700 Vietnamese civilians, and American contractors. Facilities included Danang and satellite facilities at Hue, Dong Ha, Sa Huynh, and Chu Lai. Transport responsibilities included road maintenance inside base facilities, and operation of over 350 coastal and river shipping vessels. It operated warehouses and tank farms, ice plants, and a 720-bed naval hospital.

The Marines had implemented a "pull" logistical system, in which actual usage of all commodities was tabulated in country, and requirements for shipments electronically transmitted to depots in the US and on Okinawa. Two special programs were instituted to handle the inevitable unforeseen shortages. RED BALL identified items in critically short supply in Vietnam, and arranged priority shipping from identified sources in the Western Pacific command area. CRITIPAC was a remnant of the old "push" system. The depot at Barstow, California pre-packaged 400 lb. (182kg) boxes of items likely to be "routine but rapidly expended" in combat – assorted ammunition and medical supplies – that could be held and delivered as a unit into combat.

The climate of Vietnam also helped disrupt logistical functions in ways never before seen in warfare. Early computers used by Force Logistics used paper punch cards that swelled in the high humidity, and the heat and humidity jammed the huge reel-to-reel magnetic tapes, requiring construction of climate-controlled buildings.

Force Logistics could repair virtually any damaged vehicle or equipment. Here the center at Dong Ha is repairing a badly damaged M51 tank recovery vehicle from 3rd Tank Battalion. (NARA)

Force Logistics Command was established on 15 March 1966 and by mid-1966 had ballooned from the original 700 personnel assigned to support 9th MEB to over 5,300 men. Improvements included speedier unloading of cargo at Danang, and the shifting of some fourth echelon (heavy and specialist repair) maintenance from Okinawa to Vietnam. As the war escalated and supply requirements grew, other innovations were implemented, including the use of the 3rd Force Support Regiment facility on Okinawa as a "surge tank," a sort of forward depot to accumulate supplies.

Organization

The FLC was in constant flux as the organization grew, adapting to changing military situations, before being dismantled as troops were withdrawn from Vietnam. In some cases parallel organizations at different logistical facilities in Vietnam might be differently organized. No organizational charts of this complex and ever-changing organization are truly meaningful, and in most cases the only way to determine organizational structure is by analysis of monthly unit reports. The accompanying T/Os refer to specific periods as indicated, and in some cases functions and responsibilities rather than organizational units are specified.

Day-to-day operations

In routine operations, the logistical system was both complex and flexible. The various units of FLC were responsible for the acquisition and distribution of supplies to the central facilities. From there, each of the infantry or other battalions drew supplies directly from FLC, or from one of the subordinate LSUs, and when occupying fixed positions such as firebases or encampments each company within a battalion might draw from separate facilities.

In the field the division's shore party battalion provided the direct re-supply interface with battalions, with one company supporting each infantry regiment. Shore party liaison teams (SPLT) at infantry battalion headquarters worked with

The landing zone control team was a small advanced logistical party at each landing zone, responsible for coordinating all helicopter and re-supply activities. Here a work party is loading empty plastic water bags for return to the Logistical Support Unit. (MCRC)

The seemingly mundane services provided by Force Logistics Command included laundries. This unit could process 4,000 lb. (1,800kg) per day. (MCRC)

Typical FLSG maintenance company

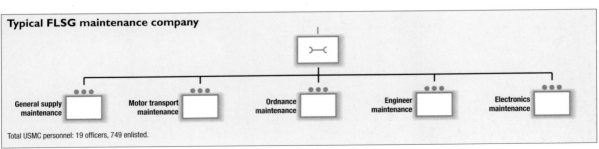

General supply maintenance | Motor transport maintenance | Ordnance maintenance | Engineer maintenance | Electronics maintenance

Total USMC personnel: 19 officers, 749 enlisted.

the battalion commander or supply officer to coordinate and assign priorities to the requisition of supplies based on the needs of the companies.

In a typical battalion support activity the SPLT would assemble and collate requests for supplies and replacement equipment, and radio the request to the infantry regiment's appropriate base support facility by 1500 hours each day. The shore party company would draw the requested materials from the LSU, assemble them into loads, and dispatch them by truck or helicopter to the battalion or company positions the next day. Helicopter support teams at each LSU assembled helicopter loads, and supervised loading. At field landing zones a landing zone control team – typically two or more shore party personnel with one or more radio operators – marked the landing zone, coordinated the arrival and departure of helicopters, briefed aircrews on details of wind and enemy activity, positioned cargo, supervised loading and unloading, and hooked up external sling loads.

Air or ground transport also carried replacement personnel to the field, and on return carried redundant or damaged gear, and unit personnel returning for various reasons.

Ramping down

Reductions in the fighting units also meant the gradual reduction of FLC's activities. In early 1970 1st Shore Party Battalion left Vietnam, leaving only C Company – attached to the 1st Engineer Battalion – to support the 1st Division. The original plan was for FLC to be deactivated in December 1970 when III MAF and 1st Division Headquarters were withdrawn (Operation *Keystone Robin Bravo*), but when the Marines were exempted, FLC was left in place and collapsed. Units were reassigned, and units like the bulk fuel, ration, communications, and ammunition companies reduced to platoons.

In March 1971 LSU-3 ceased operations. In April the headquarters of 1st FSR was officially transferred to California, though its three component battalions stayed in Danang until late June to pack and ship the mass of remaining Marine property.

Strategy and tactics

Overarching strategy

In order to understand how and why the III MAF undertook some operations, it is necessary to understand the Corps' longer-term goals. The Marines had a long-considered doctrine of how to defeat a Communist insurgency. This doctrine led to a clash with the highest American command authority in Vietnam – Military Assistance Command Vietnam (MACV) – in the person of General William C. Westmoreland.

In 1965 the Marines' immediate task was to guard the big airbase and logistical facility at Danang. They promptly set out to achieve their mission by both orthodox military means, and utilization of the *Small Wars* doctrine. Marine ground forces were at first confined to an eight-square-mile TAOR around the base: First Battalion, 3rd Marines (1/3) guarded the airbase perimeter proper, while 3/9 garrisoned small hills west of the facility. The extended hill defenses were to deny the enemy access to the so-called "rocket belt," areas within artillery rocket range of the base.

It is an article of faith with the Marines that wars are not won by defense, but by carrying the battle to the enemy. The Marines pressed for a proactive defense, and on 20 April 1965 began "aggressively patrolling" with ARVN forces beyond the TAOR. Not content to simply deny the region to large enemy units, the Marines were determined to pacify the area by denying the enemy access to the population, and the sanctuaries, food, intelligence and any other help the civilians could provide. In early May they launched their first Civic Action Program. On 4 May 2/3 sent patrols into the Le My area, a cluster of hamlets along the Cu Do River. On 11 May the battalion swept through the area in strength, arresting suspected guerrillas for questioning, and using local labor to seek out and destroy the bunkers and booby traps that infested the area.

The initial Marine strategy for countering the Communist guerrillas involved befriending the populace, developing an improved standard of living, and providing security from VC "tax collectors" at events like this chaotic local market day. (NARA)

Despite efforts to apply lessons learned from previous guerrilla wars, the Marines were forced to accept the Department of Defense and MACV's "metric" for measuring success: the body count. This led to increased emphasis on "policing up" enemy bodies. (NARA)

Close on the heels of the battalion the Regional Forces (RF) and Popular Forces (PF) units, consisting of local militiamen, were established. These were coupled with Marine Combined Action platoons who lived and worked in the villages. The CAPs and regular Marine units conducted the COUNTY FAIR program that provided medical and other assistance, and *Golden Fleece* operations that guarded the rice harvest and prevented the VC from collecting the annual "rice tax" that fed the guerrillas.

The goal was to drive the VC out of the rural population by a "spreading ink blot" strategy; the Communists would be gradually pushed back by pressure spreading from centers like Danang and Phu Bai. The CAP program rapidly expanded from 12 to 57 units by mid-1966.

In the final analysis the success of the CAP program was limited by a combination of factors. The nature of the war in the northern provinces of South Vietnam was evolving as the NVA played an increasing role. The South Vietnamese government proved incapable of permanently securing the areas the CAPs had pacified; unless Marines permanently garrisoned each village, the VC simply moved back in. Westmoreland considered pacification programs that emphasized slow and steady progress a waste of resources. Westmoreland, a hero of World War II in Europe, was wildly popular both with the political administration and the American public. He had a vision of bringing the enemy into open combat and grinding them down by superior force. Asked by a news reporter his solution to an insurgency, Westmoreland answered: "Firepower." His plan promised the immediate and measurable results desired by American political leaders.

Impatient with the Marines' model for a slow and steady elimination of the Communist forces, MACV elected to concentrate the population and declared anyone or anything in the notorious "free fire zones" a legitimate target. (NARA)

Under Westmoreland's plan, pacification was to be accomplished through the Strategic Hamlet Program. The rural population was forcibly relocated into sprawling camps separated from their farms and livestock, and from the graves of their ancestors that held immense religious significance. One could hardly have devised a program to cause greater resentment among the rural population.

In desperation, in 1966 General Krulak, the commander of FMFPAC, sought to intervene by going over Westmoreland's head to Secretary of Defense MacNamara and eventually to President Johnson. He was politely "shown the door"; the war would be fought by Westmoreland's rules.

Marine units continued to pursue a pacification program, but after 1966 they would be increasingly employed as conventional combat units in pursuit of a quick and measurable result – the body count.

Operational tactics

Prior to Vietnam the Marines had fought as divisions or even amphibious corps in fairly conventional combat. The refusal of the VC and NVA to concentrate large forces limited the scale of the Marine units that it was practical to deploy against them to battalions or brigades, and Marine formations were often obliged to further limit the manpower deployed in any operation by the necessity to protect rear areas and base camps.

Vietnam saw another change in Marine Corps operational practices, that of cross-attaching units. Traditionally single regiments, with a single clear chain of command, conducted major operations. By combining elements of two regiments, headquarters could achieve greater tactical flexibility – but at a cost to efficiency. Commanders and subordinates might be unfamiliar, the officers and men of units in the line might not know their neighbors, and units as small as platoons attached to other formations sometimes created a confused chain of command. Operation *Starlite* in 1965 established the precedent, and the practice continued throughout the war.

Area sweeps, or "search and destroy" operations, were large-scale encirclements, usually conducted in battalion or brigade strength. These operations were intended to locate and destroy VC forces identified by intelligence, or to disrupt enemy activities and destroy base areas and logistics. Composite forces of as many as four rifle battalions attempted to encircle, fix, and destroy the enemy. Rapid mobility provided by helicopters or vehicles was a key element. Typically a part of the force would be transported into position to block enemy escape or retreat, while the balance deployed in a broad line to sweep through and clear a specific area. By 1969 some of these operations were conducted by reinforced brigades.

In the mountainous interior of northernmost South Vietnam, the 3rd Marine Division fought a more conventional war against the NVA. The NVA established base areas covering hundreds of square kilometers, complete with major logistical sites, field hospitals, artillery bases, training areas, and many of the other accouterments of a conventional army. Multi-trunk telephone lines and a dense network of trails knitted the complexes together. Weapons included conventional artillery complete with trucks and tracked prime movers for the big guns, and anti-aircraft artillery.

Operations against these remote base areas required more conventional tactics, with brigade-sized infantry forces advancing on a broad front supported by artillery. The mountainous terrain limited the use of ground transport and armor, so such operations made extensive use of helicopters as both tactical and logistical transport. Helicopters would transport infantry deep into hostile territory to seize key terrain objectives. Combat engineers, sometimes equipped with air-transportable bulldozers, would quickly move in to construct artillery firebases. Close on their heels logistical units moved forward to establish supply points, with ammunition, food and water all transported by helicopter.

Additional infantry, supported by the fire of the artillery, would then secure nearby objectives, and the process would be repeated. The advance was similar to a "broad front" advance in traditional warfare, with helicopters substituting for conventional transport. The key to this type of mobile warfare was to always advance under the protective cover of artillery.

Fire support

Ever since World War II, the artillery has been the backbone of American ground firepower. The flexibility of the artillery system was such that direct support guns could also fire in support of other units. The fire of the more powerful 155mm guns was allocated by the division's Artillery Fire Coordination center.

Marine units were supported not only by the light and medium howitzers and heavy mortars of their own divisional artillery battalions, but by corps-level artillery including 8in. (208mm) howitzers and 155mm or later 175mm guns. The long-range 175mm guns could not fire their missions in close proximity to infantry because of the considerable dispersion of the round impacts at long ranges. Army artillery units also supported Marine divisions.

The Marines utilized the firepower of fleet units offshore, including 5in. (127mm) quick-firing guns of destroyers, 8in. (208mm) cruiser guns, and even 16in. (416mm) guns from Iowa-class battleships. Naval firepower was controlled by detachments from ANGLICOs, equipped with long-range radios to communicate directly with aircraft and naval units offshore.

The lavish use of artillery was one of the salient aspects of the war. On the offensive, portable and reliable radio communications reaching down to platoon or even squad level gave Marines in the field access to unprecedented firepower. The ability to adjust fire by quickly relaying requests through a chain of command or communicating directly with artillery units meant that such firepower could be brought to bear on specific targets rather than broad area fires or pre-plotted targets. In the offensive, artillery was not used simply to suppress the defense. Infantry units that found themselves in trouble – repulsed in an attack or caught in an ambush – could call upon artillery to help extricate them.

Curtains of artillery fire were a fundamental part of the defense. Infantry fire coordinators (typically a task of the infantry company executive officer) or forward observers accompanying infantry units could pre-plot defensive fires along likely paths of approach or assembly areas that might be used by the enemy.

In both offense and defense artillery and mortar fire was typically called in as a map coordinate. In poorly mapped areas the artillery "pre-registered" by firing one or more HE or WP smoke rounds at some terrain feature, with the observer moving the impact by advising the Artillery Fire Direction Center to shift fire. Later fire missions could then be adjusted by training the guns relative to the known registration point.

In a typical fire mission the forward observer specified the type of target and location as closely as could be determined. The artillery battery firing in support would issue the fire mission, specifying ammunition type (typically HE or WP), number of rounds, and fuse. The battery would fire one registration round, and the observer would adjust the impact. When a round struck the desired target, the command "fire for effect" released the guns to deliver the specified number of rounds in as short a period as possible to achieve maximum shock effect. In a sustained attack, the guns fired at a slower rate to avoid overheating.

A more complex artillery tactic was the box barrage. Several batteries were used to lay down curtains of artillery fire along three sides of a square, while the fire of another battery formed the fourth side, and swept to and fro to devastate anything caught inside the box. Controlled Fragmentation Munitions (COFRAM) rounds, artillery shells that burst open to scatter bomblets that detonated a meter off the ground, were first used at Khe Sanh to form the rolling "piston" in a box barrage.

Specific artillery tactics also included the Time-on-Target mission, in which several batteries fired at the same target. The guns fired at different times, with flight times for the rounds calculated to make the impacts simultaneous. The psychological and shock effect of this type of strike was enormous.

More controversial were Harassment and Interdiction (H&I) missions. Specific geographic locations, such as trail intersections, transportation choke-points, and other locations likely to be used by the enemy were targeted for random bombardment. As indicated by the name, the purpose of these missions was as much to interfere with military activities as to inflict casualties. In some operations H&I fires were replaced by "Moving Target Fire," missions based on information from airdropped seismic sensors that detected the vibrations and voices of moving men.

Air Force, Navy, and Marine Corps fighter-bomber units provided direct tactical air support, controlled by infantry commanders, air liaison units operating with the ground troops, or by forward air controllers in light aircraft. In general ground units preferred support provided by Marine aviation, as they were more specifically trained and experienced in the support role. Typical air-delivered munitions included napalm, ballistic "iron bombs," SNAKEYE bombs with drag fins that allowed a low-flying aircraft to escape the blast of its own bombs, and strafing with 20mm cannon.

The most powerful bombardment was ARC LIGHT, the code name for high-altitude area bombing, usually by six Air Force B-52s. Because of the long flight time from bases outside Vietnam, strikes were arranged at least 15 hours in advance, but could be redirected on three hours' notice. During the siege of Khe Sanh in 1968, it was necessary for the NVA to concentrate troops and logistics in known areas or areas detectable by reconnaissance. Eight strikes in each 24-hour period were the norm. The massive bomb load churned an area about one by three kilometers, blasting huge craters. Chances of survival for anyone caught in the strike were minimal, and ARC LIGHT strikes were not delivered within 1,000m of friendly troops. Mini- ARC LIGHT and micro- ARC LIGHT were non-visual strikes delivered by high-flying A-6 Intruders or F-4 Phantoms.

Small-unit infantry tactics

In the final analysis Vietnam was a small-unit war, and the rifle squad and platoon were the most fundamental units in the fighting organization. The principles around which the Corps constructed its small-unit doctrine were simple tactics and aggressive assault. This combination was sometimes derided as a "hey diddle-diddle, right up the middle" mentality that produced unnecessarily heavy casualties. The Marines believed that simplicity creates less deadly confusion in combat, and that aggressive and rapid destruction of the enemy ultimately minimizes losses.

Whether on squad- or platoon-size routine patrols, or in larger "search and destroy" sweeps conducted by several companies, the basic movement formation was the column. The concept had not changed much since the American Civil War, and was designed to prevent the main force from stumbling into an enemy ambush unawares.

A typical platoon column deployed a fire team from the leading squad as an advance party, with one lone scout "walking point" to detect enemy ambushes.

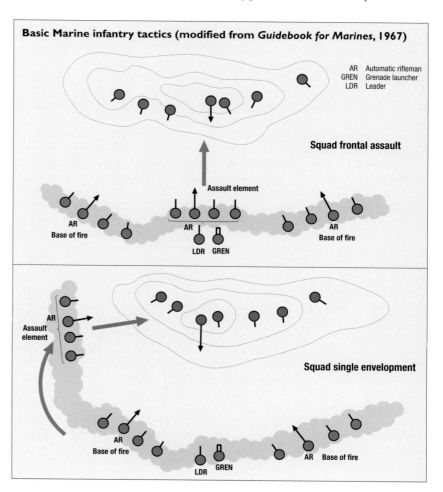

Basic Marine infantry tactics (modified from *Guidebook for Marines*, 1967)

AR Automatic rifleman
GREN Grenade launcher
LDR Leader

Squad frontal assault

Assault element

AR
Base of fire

AR

LDR GREN

AR
Base of fire

AR
Assault element

Squad single envelopment

AR
Base of fire

LDR GREN

AR Base of fire

This advance group was separated from the main body by up to 50m in close terrain; the separation was to try to assure that both the advance party and the main body could not be enveloped in a single ambush. The main body included the command group and the balance of the three squads. Another fire team detailed from the last squad trailed the column to provide rear security. Larger company columns might deploy squad-sized flanking elements, but this was often not practical as it slowed movement.

When the enemy was located, Marine doctrine emphasized two basic tactics for assault of enemy positions. The column deployed to a line formation in order to bring maximum firepower to bear. In a typical squad assault two fire teams and the M79 grenadier provided a base of fire to suppress enemy return fire and fix his attention. M60 machine gun sections seconded from the company weapons platoon supplemented the platoon or squad's firepower. Fire from 60mm or 81mm mortars or artillery could be called upon to help suppress the defense. Depending upon terrain and understanding of the defenses, the third element assaulted the position by frontal assault (direct assault), or by moving around one flank (single envelopment), with other elements following once the position was penetrated. Basic platoon and company tactics were simply scaled up versions of squad tactics.

Small units assaulted by "bounds," or short alternating rushes. In fire-team bounds, one fire team moved, covered by fire from the others, then went to ground and provided covering fire for another team to advance. In individual rushes, alternating pairs of men moved, covered by the other members of the fire team.

In the defense of temporary positions, usually at night, each unit established a perimeter for all-around defense, with each subunit assigned a sector of the circle. Marines were taught to construct fairly complex two-man fighting holes, complete with protective berms, firing steps, and grenade sumps. Establishing night defenses at late hours, the fact that on a sweep positions would be occupied no more than a single night, the burden of re-supply and weapons maintenance, and simple fatigue discouraged elaborate works. In practice, the infantry seldom constructed more than rudimentary pits, or took advantage of irregularities in the ground for protection. In more established defenses trench lines were more common.

Individuals were assigned a small sector of the defensive circle to observe and defend, and one method of defining their individual arc was to position sticks or other objects to limit the swing of the rifle in the darkness. In the defense the machine gun sections reverted to the weapons platoon, whose commander positioned them to defend the most threatened sectors. Depending upon the situation small patrols might be sent out to establish ambushes. Listening posts (small units positioned forward of the defenses to provide advanced warning of enemy approach) were not as extensively used as in prior conflicts because of the lavish use of artillery and air support in the defense.

Urban combat

As a result of experience in towns and villages during World War II, and the fighting for the city of Seoul in 1950, Marines were taught simple urban combat skills in ITR. The fighting in Hue during the 1968 Tet Offensive utilized some of these principles, but other tactics had to be improvised.

A basic modification to the squad assault was to divide the squad into a searching party and a covering party of two fire teams each. Under protective fire from the covering party, the searching party invaded the building, if possible by attaining the upper floors and fighting downward. Extensive use was made of grenades to clear rooms, and demolitions to blow "mouse holes" through walls to gain access. Since most defenders will fight more desperately if trapped, in principle the searching team tried to drive defenders out and into an observed killing zone established by the covering party.

The sturdy masonry construction and walled gardens made each house and building in the Imperial City of Hue a mini-fortress. The bullet-pocked trees and walls attest to the violence of the street fighting. (NARA)

In Hue the VC and NVA defenders took full advantage of the broad boulevards on the south, or French colonial, side of the city to establish broad fields of fire. The Marines quickly learned to advance through the back gardens of the large houses, blasting gaps through the masonry walls. In one case tanks were used to crush paths through walls and flimsy buildings to establish an enclosed, safe pathway between the casualty clearing station and the only helicopter-landing site.

Tanks and Ontos provided direct fire in assaults. The HE round fired by the M48A3 tank's 90mm gun would blast holes in walls, or penetrate to explode inside enemy-occupied rooms. The High Explosive Plastic Tracer (HEP-T) round fired by the Ontos's 106mm recoilless gun flattened into a "pancake" on impact, and then detonated, making it very useful for blowing access holes through masonry walls.

One other weapon used extensively in Hue was CS tear gas, used as a harassing agent to suppress defenses and – rarely – to force the enemy into the open. This agent was delivered by air dropped canister, grenades, or ground-emplaced riot control launchers.

The Combined Action Program

The basic unit of the CAP was the abbreviated 12-man squad. These units were staffed entirely with volunteers, who on many occasions extended their 13-month tour of duty to remain in "their" village. These units lived in the village, often in a semi-fortified compound with locals of the Regional or Popular Forces, ate the local food, and conducted improvement projects. Their primary tactical operations were small patrols and nocturnal ambushes to disrupt Communist infiltration efforts.

Combined Action units were equipped with radio communications, and could call upon mortar or artillery fire support. However, only the CAP units could call in such fires in areas under CAP control. In emergency the squads or platoons could request assistance from regular infantry units.

Combat reserves

The availability of rapid helicopter transport generally made it unnecessary to hold an operational reserve in immediate proximity to the fighting. The operational reserve for most operations was a unit in a base camp, or one of the Special Landing Force battalions offshore. These units were usually placed on stand-by notification, to be ready to move at short notice.

Marine units in Vietnam had no deep reserve system under which large formations could be withdrawn as units for recuperation. The closest approximation was the 1st Division's "Stack Arms" Center at China Beach south of Danang, where infantry companies could spend 48 hours swimming in the ocean, wolfing down hot food and cold beer, and just relaxing in a relatively safe environment. Individual battalions rotated in and out of combat in order to recuperate and integrate replacements for casualties and transfers, but during such recuperation periods a unit would still be called upon to undertake local security duties including active and aggressive patrolling. As noted, during a major operation a "resting" infantry unit, usually a company or a battalion, would be placed on standby as an operational reserve to be quickly committed to action.

Infantry units that were exhausted or badly battered in combat would commonly be pulled out to recuperate by providing base area security or some

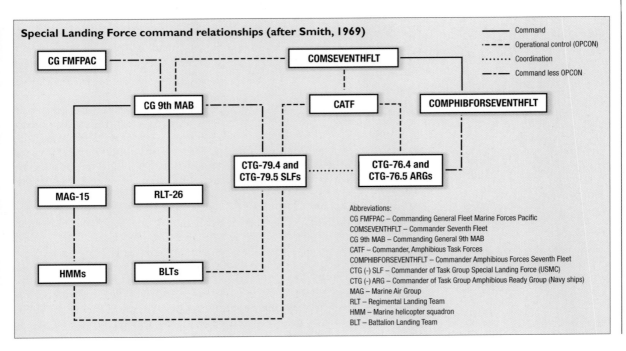

Special Landing Force command relationships (after Smith, 1969)

Abbreviations:
CG FMFPAC – Commanding General Fleet Marine Forces Pacific
COMSEVENTHFLT – Commander Seventh Fleet
CG 9th MAB – Commanding General 9th MAB
CATF – Commander, Amphibious Task Forces
COMPHIBFORSEVENTHFLT – Commander Amphibious Forces Seventh Fleet
CTG (-) SLF – Commander of Task Group Special Landing Force (USMC)
CTG (-) ARG – Commander of Task Group Amphibious Ready Group (Navy ships)
MAG – Marine Air Group
RLT – Regimental Landing Team
HMM – Marine helicopter squadron
BLT – Battalion Landing Team

similar function. In practice this was limited by the limited availability of operational reserves, and the psychological ability of Marine units to continue to function in the face of heavy casualties.

In theory the Special Landing Forces under Seventh Fleet provided a theatre reserve. However, the Special Landing Forces had to stand ready to intervene in a crisis anywhere within the Southeast Asia–South China Sea region. Furthermore, confused command relationships made the MEUs less than fully effective as a floating reserve for III MAF. With the Special Landing Forces under Seventh Fleet as opposed to III MAF control, it was typically more efficient to utilize units internal to III MAF.

Personnel replacement

Unlike previous conflicts, Marine units had to operate with their personnel in constant flux. In World War II the high casualty rates – up to 70 percent – in major campaigns led to the institution of pre-positioned replacement drafts. At Iwo Jima and Okinawa up to three large drafts (1,250 officers and men was typical) were attached to each division. These men served as shore party and cargo handlers for the division until needed to replace combat losses.[4]

The institution of a rotation policy in the Korean War required a continuous "pipeline" replacement system, with men flowing in and out. This system was used in Vietnam, where the normal tour of duty was fixed at 13 months for Marines.

Records were used to estimate the number and MOS mix of personnel required to replace anticipated combat losses, losses to other causes like disease or accident, and men who had completed their tour of duty. Replacements

4 See Battle Orders 8: *US Marine Corps Pacific Theatre of Operations 1944–45*

arrived at Danang in planeload batches aboard Freedom Birds – charted civilian airliners. At Danang they were processed through a central replacement center, then utilized as working parties to support the sprawling base while they acclimated to the intense heat and poor sanitation.

Eventually men would be assigned in response to unit requests for replacements. Smaller groups of replacements worked their way through a series of destinations, traveling by air or ground transport through division, regimental, and battalion headquarters. Eventually the replacement arrived at his unit, where he was slotted into a particular position. The rotation policy meant that the new man might be completely inexperienced, a combat veteran of a previous war, or might have served one or more prior tours of duty in Vietnam. He might be a private, or a senior officer. The entire composition of every unit at every level unit, from squad to division, was constantly in change, and every unit was guaranteed to change in its entirety within the 13 months specified by an individual's tour of duty. This was aggravated by the rapid rotation of officers (see *Command and control*).

Individual replacements would often be brought into the unit during an active operation, like food, ammunition, or any other supply. Still, the inevitable lag between the time a man was killed or wounded and the arrival of his replacement, and the equally inevitable absences of men on R&R (a brief mid-tour leave), sick call, absent for training, and the loss of personnel requisitioned for rear-area duties, meant that front-line combat units were consistently below their authorized strength.

An unintended consequence of the rotation policy was a deleterious effect on morale and combat efficiency. The most experienced men were constantly drained out and often replaced by novices. Since combat mortality is usually highest among inexperienced replacements, in periods of intense combat older hands might be reluctant to establish relationships with someone who might only survive for a few days. This was not intentional cruelty, just the more experienced men protecting themselves from even more psychological injury. As a man approached the end of his tour, he often became understandably reluctant to risk being killed or maimed. It was also considered very bad for the unit as a whole to lose a "short-timer."

Weapons

In its longest war the Corps used a wide variety of weapons. A few pre-dated World War I, while others introduced during the war still serve into the 21st century. Most were standardized with the Army, but as always a few were unique to the Marines in their role as amphibious and air mobile light infantry. The Marines were the last to use ground-based flame weapons, but the heavy logistical burden and the availability of air-delivered weapons like napalm caused flame weapons to fall into disfavor.

The Marines can lay claim to having pioneered the concept of a combined arms team, but in contrast to many armies Marine Corps doctrine is clear that the primary role of all arms is infantry support. To this end, the Corps provides the infantry with massive firepower that is, as far as possible, directly controlled by the infantry commander.

Opposing weapons

When the Marines entered Vietnam, they expected an asymmetrical war against lightly equipped local guerrillas. Some local VC units were in fact equipped with a ragtag assortment of World War II-era weapons captured from the French and South Vietnamese, supplied by the Allies to fight the Japanese in World War II, captured by the Communist Chinese in their own civil war, and from many other sources. The Marines also faced the NVA, a disciplined and highly motivated regular army equipped with modern small arms and heavy weapons.

After local VC units were decimated in the disastrous Tet Offensive of early 1968, the NVA assumed the main burden of the fighting in I Corps. The NVA made skilful use of most conventional weapons systems including artillery and on occasion even tanks, despite complete American air superiority.

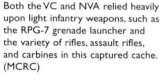
Both the VC and NVA relied heavily upon light infantry weapons, such as the RPG-7 grenade launcher and the variety of rifles, assault rifles, and carbines in this captured cache. (MCRC)

The standard infantry weapons of the NVA were the rugged and reliable Soviet-designed 7.62mm AK-47 assault rifle, and the SKS (Chinese Type 56) rifle. Various models of the Rocket Propelled Grenade launcher (RPG) were common as antitank and direct fire explosive weapons, filling the niche of the rocket and grenade launchers used by the Marines. The RPG-7 was the most modern and deadly, but older models were in common use. NVA units were equipped with crew-served weapons including light machine guns (the Soviet RPD and Chinese Type 85 were common) and heavy machine guns (12.7mm and 14.5mm caliber weapons), and mortars (the 82mm and 120mm were most common). The 82mm B-10 (Chinese Type 65) and older 75mm and 57mm recoilless guns were far more powerful than the RPGs, and could readily destroy American tanks.

The NVA used rocket artillery, both from ordinary wheeled or truck-mounted launchers, and fired from portable launchers. Rocket artillery was far more mobile than tube artillery since the individual rockets and portable launchers could be man-carried through rough terrain impassable to wheeled guns and tractors, and more easily concealed from American airpower. The most common rockets were 107mm and 122mm caliber.

The NVA also fielded Soviet-made tube artillery of 122mm, 130mm, and 152mm calibers. Shelling of Marine positions along the DMZ from guns north of the border commenced in 1967, and was a grim fact of existence in the DMZ positions occupied by the 3rd Marine Division. These guns easily outranged the American artillery. The 152mm gun had a maximum range of 17,260m, some 2,300m greater than the Marines' long-range general support weapon, the 155mm howitzer. The 130mm long-range gun fired a 74 lb. (33kg) round to 31,000m, over twice the range of the 155mm. At the siege of Khe Sanh the NVA emplaced guns on the Co Roc hill massif inside Laos, and shelled the combat base with relative impunity.

The NVA possessed as many as 600 PT-76, T-54 and T-55 tanks, plus Soviet BTR-60 and Chinese Type 531 armored personnel carriers. Though the Marines were prepared to deal with enemy tanks, the NVA made little use of them against American forces.

Individual weapons

The backbone of Marine fighting formations was the infantryman, and in the early days of the war his standard weapon was the semi-automatic 7.62mm M14 rifle. This heavy (11.1 lb./5kg fully loaded), gas actuated weapon was superseded by the lighter (7.6 lb./3.5kg) 5.56m M16 rifle. The M14 remained in service as a heavy sniper weapon and the weapon of choice for some Marines. Enormous psychological emphasis was placed upon the rifleman and his role as the Marine who aggressively closes with and destroys the enemy. From the first day of training, all Marines were indoctrinated with the concept that the rifle is the primary Marine weapon.

The standard sidearm for officers and crew-served weapons operators was the .45-caliber M1911A1 automatic pistol. Difficult to master, this monster was renowned for both its brutal recoil and its stopping power.

The rifle squad leader's dedicated support weapon was the M79 grenade launcher. The stubby break-action M79 fired a 40mm HE round out to 410 yards

The M79 grenade launcher gave the squad leader a high-explosive fire capability, combining aspects of the old rifle grenade and a light mortar. This grenadier is bringing plunging fire down on enemy trenches during Operation *Chinook*, 1967. (MCRC)

The M16 rifle controversy

In a controversial war, few things created greater controversy than the M16 rifle. Introduced in 1967, it was lighter than the older M14 and in theory the smaller round would allow each soldier or Marine to carry nearly twice the previous load of ammunition. The M16 immediately generated one of the great scandals of the war.

The low weight of the new rifle was in part achieved by incorporating many plastic parts. Marines accustomed to using the massive metal butt plate of the M14 for such tasks as hammering down doors broke more than a few, but the real problem lay in a radically new operating system.

The M14 used a small part of the propellant gas, extracted from the barrel near the front, to actuate a cylinder-and-rod assembly that moved the bolt to the rear and chambered the next round. Used gas, with any unburned powder and residue it carried, was expelled through a port at the lower front of the weapon. In other respects the M14 was also a "luxury model" weapon, with chromium plated chamber and bore. The hardened surfaces made it very forgiving, and it would function well even if fouled with dirt and debris.

In the M16, activating gas was ducted through a tube that ran back atop the barrel, then vented into a small cup on top of the bolt assembly; this puff of gas drove the bolt to the rear, but vented directly into the bolt housing (Warrior No. 23, *US Marine in Vietnam* includes a schematic of the weapon). The residue of unburned powder would not only build up on the bolt face, but would trap dirt and debris and drive it into the chamber, which lacked the chromium plating. The problem was further exacerbated by the use of a lower and more corrosive grade of powder than originally specified. To make things even worse, a rumor circulated that the weapon was "self-cleaning," and did not require constant maintenance.

The end result of this chain of problems was that the softer metal of the M16s chamber would become pitted both by corrosive residue and the abrasive dust and fine sand it trapped. Eventually the rifle would jam when a spent cartridge case failed to extract, and the rifleman would have to try and ram the casing out with a metal bore cleaning rod. In extreme cases the extractors that plucked the casing out would instead rip it apart, leaving the larger piece in the bore and rendering the rifle useless. The new rifle acquired a hateful reputation, and it became policy in Marine units to test fire all weapons before each patrol, further depleting critical ammunition supplies.

Once the problems were identified, Force Logistics Command recalled and modified all weapons in country, and the M16 went on to become a reliable and widely used weapon still in service today. (Photo: NARA)

(375m), and gave the squad leader his own means of bringing immediate HE fire down on a target. It also fired marker smoke and canister (shotgun) rounds.

The egg-shaped M26 and M26A1 fragmentation grenades, and the smaller spherical M67 grenade, were far deadlier than their World War II counterparts. A powerful bursting charge fragmented a serrated coiled wire inside the body and hurled fragments as far as 185m, though the effective kill radius (the limit beyond which the fragment dispersal did not assure several strikes on a human body) was considered to be 15m. Other grenades in common use included the Mk2 Illumination, AN-M14 Incendiary, M15 White Phosphorus Smoke, M18 Colored Smoke (red, green, violet, and yellow), and the M7 or M7A1 CN tear-gas grenade.

The Marine also carried a bayonet for his M14 or M16 rifle, and a large fighting knife (generically called a Ka-Bar, after the most popular manufacturer) in a brown or black leather sheath. Training with the bayonet and knife was intended as much to instill an aggressive attitude as to prepare for close combat.

The M1912 riot gun was a militarized 12-gauge pump-action shotgun with sling, hand guard over the barrel, and a bayonet lug. It was issued in limited numbers. One rarely seen weapon was the M3A1 "Grease Gun" submachine gun, a World War II vintage weapon that used the same ammunition as the .45-caliber pistol. Inaccurate and hard to maintain, it was still issued as a personal weapon for tank crews.

Crew-served weapons

The M19 60mm mortar with M4 sight equipped the infantry company mortar section. The 45.2 lb. (20.5kg) weapon fired HE, WP smoke, and illuminating rounds out to a maximum range of 1,985 yards (HE round), with a sustained rate of fire of 18 rounds per minute. The illumination round had a fixed time fuse that exploded 15 seconds after firing. Though the 3 lb. (1.36kg) HE round lacked the penetration and explosive power of the 81mm mortar, it could be brought into action quickly, and the 100-yard minimum range made it useful for close-in fighting.

The M29 81mm mortar with M34A2 sight was the infantry battalion commander's "pocket artillery." This 115 lb. (52kg) weapon fired HE, WP smoke, and illumination rounds out to a maximum range of 4,940 yards (1,500m), with a sustained rate of fire of 18 rounds per minute. Both types of weapons were deployed as far forward as possible and employed aggressively, since they provided the most immediately available firepower.

The 7.62mm M60 machine gun replaced several types previously used, and was the infantry company's heavy firepower. It weighed 24 lb. (10.9kg), with an additional 33 lb. (15kg) of accessories and ready ammunition carried by the assistant gunner. Two ammunition men carried cans with more belted ammunition, which weighed 6½ lb. (3kg) per 100 round belt. It was a deadly and reliable weapon, with higher cyclic and sustained rates of fire than earlier machine guns. The M60s of the company weapons section provided the commander with flexible firepower that could be either parceled out at platoon or squad level, or concentrated for massed fire.

The M2 series .50-caliber heavy machine gun was primarily used as a vehicle-mounted weapon, though some were mounted on tripods and used for long-range fire in static defenses. The .50-caliber was extremely powerful, but had a slow rate of fire and without proper adjustment of the recoil head spacing could malfunction.

Infantry antitank weapons were used primarily in the direct-fire role when assaulting enemy-occupied buildings, bunkers, and other fortified positions. The 3½in. (89mm) rocket launcher "Super Bazooka" was sometimes used for indirect fire. Primary munitions were the M28A2 HEAT and WP smoke rockets, which weighed 8.61 lb. (3.91kg) each. The heavy, bulky rocket launcher was largely replaced by the 4.34 lb. (2kg) 66mm-caliber M72 Light Antitank Assault Weapon (LAAW) with its disposable launcher. This weapon was issued to individual riflemen.

The man portable M2A1 flamethrower was used in small numbers – about two per battalion. The M2A1 would fire a burst of flame for up to 40 yards (31.5m) with thickened fuel. Although effective in clearing bunkers and tunnels, its considerable weight (68 to 72 lb., or 31 to 33kg), limited duration of fire (six to nine seconds per charge), and appetite for special fuel and propellant gas were severe tactical liabilities.

The older 3½in. "Super Bazooka" was in part replaced by the Light Antitank Assault Weapon, but remained in service for its enormous explosive power and variety of rounds.

The 106mm recoilless rifle was used by the infantry antitank platoons and some artillery units. It could be mounted on a tripod, or on the small M274 "Mechanical Mule" utility vehicles used by the infantry battalion's H&S company. It was also the main armament of the M50 Ontos tank destroyer of the antitank battalion. The 106mm fired antitank, high-explosive, and antipersonnel "beehive" rounds. One round, the HEP-T, was particularly effective at breaching masonry or concrete walls.

Artillery

Although Marine doctrine emphasizes infantry combat to an extent that it is often criticized as being a "cult of infantry," artillery was one of the division's most effective killers. Used lavishly, and controlled by efficient communications, it was used to shock and suppress the enemy in the attack. In the defense, the "steel rain" of artillery airbursts inflicted crippling casualties on enemy formations.

The Marines utilized several artillery pieces that were unique to them – both older weapons that had been retired from Army service, and the unusual M30 Howtar mortar-gun hybrid developed especially for the Marines.

The M101A1 105mm howitzer, which entered service in World War II, was the main armament of the three (1st through 3rd) direct support battalions of the regiment. The 105 could throw its 33 lb. (15kg) projectile out to a maximum range of 12,500 yards (11,428m), and typically fired HE or WP smoke with a variety of quick (impact), variable time (VT), or proximity detonated fuses. The standard tow vehicle was a 2½ ton 6x6 truck, but the piece could be airlifted by helicopter.

The Howtar hybrid

It is often and mistakenly believed that the Marine Corps utilized castoff and redundant Army equipment, but in accordance with its stated mission the Corps developed many unique items from uniforms to amphibian tractors. The M98 Howtar is one of the least-known examples.

In the late 1930s the Marine Corps adopted the 75mm M1A1 pack howitzer as the standard direct support artillery piece for the new Fleet Marine Force. Designed as a mountain gun that could be disassembled and transported by pack mules, the pack howitzer served primarily with Marine and Army airborne divisions. Later versions had pneumatic tires for towing behind vehicles, and it could be folded up into a compact mass

for towing or loading into an assault glider. In firing position the hinged box trail "broke" in the middle to sit on the ground for greater stability. For the Marines the advantage was that it could be manhandled ashore or into rough terrain if the need arose. The little howitzers were gradually phased out in favor of the more powerful 105mm howitzer, but served until 1945.

The recommendations of the 1956 Hogaboom Board called for divisional artillery batteries to be re-equipped with the bipod-mounted 4.2in. (107mm) M30 rifled mortar. This piece could be disassembled and weighed less than a fifth of the 105mm howitzer's 4,260 lb. (1,934kg). The bursting power of the mortar's high explosive round was essentially equivalent to the howitzer,

but it had a shorter range. Disadvantages were the heavy baseplate, and the necessity to assemble the big weapon, which made it slow to bring into action. The Hogaboom Board's recommendations were never fully implemented, but each direct support artillery battalion received a battery of the M30 mortars.

The M98 Howtar was a hybrid that combined the best characteristics of the mortar and the light 75mm gun carriage. The thin-walled mortar tube was adapted to the gun cradle, and the box trail shortened. The resulting weapon was helicopter transportable, quick to bring into action, could be towed by a vehicle or disassembled and carried by men, had a shorter minimum range than the bipod mount (an advantage in jungle warfare), and greater accuracy at long ranges as a result of the more stable mount.

In 1962 the Corps adopted the M98 as a standard weapon, equipping one six-gun battery in each direct support artillery battalion.

The accompanying photograph shows a Howtar in position during Operation *Deckhouse IV*, conducted by Task Force Delta and the Special Landing Force in Quang Tri Province, September 1966. The object on the ground in front of the gun is the receiver group and pintle of a .50-caliber machine gun, lying upside down.

The 4th or general support battalion of each regiment was primarily equipped with the towed M1A1 155mm howitzer. This heavier piece, also a descendant of a World War II weapon, fired a 98 lb. (44.5kg) projectile to a maximum range of 16,350 yards (14,955m). The variety of fuses was the same as for the 105mm howitzer. The prime mover was the five-ton truck. The M109 was the lightly armored, self-propelled variant with the 155mm howitzer mounted in a turret with 360-degree traverse. The Marines had anticipated that this vehicle would fully replace the towed gun, with all 155mm howitzers assigned to Force Troops. In Vietnam the M109 equipped individual batteries in the general support battalions.

The M98 Howtar was developed by the Marine Corps as a small, lightweight, and highly mobile piece that could provide large-caliber, high-angle plunging fire in direct support of infantry operations. The M30 84.2in. mortar that served as the basis for the Howtar was also used, and both weapons were assigned to the mortar battery of each direct support artillery battalion.

The Marines retained the last of the self-propelled long-range 155mm guns, the M53, which mounted the long-tube gun in a turret set far aft on a 50-ton chassis. The huge M53 utilized many common parts with the M48 and M103 series tanks. The same chassis and turret fitted with the 8in. (203mm) howitzer was known as the M55. This 8in. howitzer was one of the most accurate field pieces ever deployed by American forces, capable of delivering its 200 lb. (91kg) projectile with great accuracy at ranges of 18,000 yards (14.2km). The newer 175mm M107 and 8in. M110 self-propelled guns eventually replaced both types. These heavier guns were Force Troops weapons, not generally assigned at division level, and in Vietnam they were part of the Field Artillery Group.

In the final months of the war some units received small numbers of the Army's M108, a 105mm howitzer mounted in the same chassis and turret as the M109. This weapon was never popular, being "too much chassis for too little gun."

Tanks and tank destroyers

In contrast to other combat arms, where they could legitimately lay claim to innovative and sophisticated doctrine, the Marines never developed a viable armor doctrine. Tanks in particular were typically employed as penny-packets of platoon and even two-tank sections in support of infantry formations.

The M48A3 was armed with a 90mm main gun and two machine guns: a .30-caliber coaxial, and a .50-caliber inside an armored cupola. The peculiar mounting of the cupola gun, lying on its side, caused jamming problems, and 1st Tank Battalion vehicles usually remounted the gun outside the cupola in a "sky mount." The 3rd Tank Battalion deployed along the DMZ retained the cupola gun because the intensive fighting against powerful NVA units made "sky mount" guns too dangerous.

The M67 flame tank was unique to the Marine Corps. Externally almost identical to the M48A3, the 90mm was replaced by a powerful flame gun that fired thickened fuel ("napalm"). Though effective against enemy defenses, the required support – gasoline for the flame gun as opposed to the tank's diesel, compressed gas for propellant, and special support vehicles such as mixing trucks – placed a heavy burden on logistics, and it was not popular with tank unit commanders.

The M50 Ontos tank destroyer that equipped the antitank battalions mounted six 106mm recoilless guns and a special .50-caliber spotting rifle on a light tracked chassis. The spotting rifle was a single-shot device, and did not fire the same round as the .50-caliber machine gun. Though possessed of considerable firepower, it was very lightly armored and vulnerable to both anti-armor weapons and machine gun fire. It was used primarily because it provided some mobility for the 106mm gun.

Amphibian tractors

The most uniquely Marine vehicle, the large box-like LVTP-5, carried up to 34 infantry, though 25 was the optimal load. It was more often used as an infantry and cargo transport on land, a role to which it was poorly suited, as the numerous small road wheels tended to shed their rims during prolonged land operation. The fuel cells for the gasoline engine were mounted in the floor, rendering it vulnerable to mines, a favorite Communist weapon. As a result the infantry often chose to ride on top, rather than to risk incineration inside.

The amtrac was armed with a single .30-caliber machine gun in a cupola, so the crews often constructed "gun pits" of sandbags and occasionally steel culvert on the upper deck, containing additional light and heavy machine guns, or even 106mm recoilless guns.

The command vehicle variant was essentially identical, but equipped with numerous rack-mounted radios and map boards necessary for communications and command functions. It was distinguishable by the numerous additional antennae. The LVTE-1 engineer/breaching vehicle carried a large front-mounted mine plow and a rocket-propelled explosive line charge launcher for breaching minefields.

The LVTH-6A1, also referred to as the LVT-6, was the last of the armed amphibians, with a gyrostabilized M49 105mm howitzer in an armored turret. Though considered an indirect fire artillery weapon, it was more often used as an improvised tank in the direct fire role, particularly in flooded areas inaccessible to tanks.

The most common variant of the LVTP-5A1 amphibian tractor was the LVTE-1 engineer/breaching vehicle, with its distinctive mine plow mounted on the front. The thinly armored amtracs tried to keep the front of the vehicle, with the double steel walls and internal flotation tank of the passenger ramp, toward the enemy.

Command, control, communications, and intelligence

Command and control

The peculiar nature of the long war in Vietnam brought about a profound change in command relationships between junior enlisted men and senior officers and senior career non-commissioned officers (the latter two often derided as "lifers"). The change in relationship was not for the better, and damaged the Corps more than is commonly realized.

As a relatively small elite force, the Corps had always prided itself on personal leadership, from generals to enlisted men. Certain officers and NCOs were legendary, men like Dan Daly, "Red Mike" Edson, Evan Carlson, "Howling Mad" Smith, and the ultimate Marine, Lewis Burwell "Chesty" Puller. Puller exemplified the traits that would allow Marines to admire the men who would lead them to their deaths. An enlisted man who rose to the rank of lieutenant general, Puller was widely admired by enlisted men because he looked out for the welfare of his men, and joined them in their hardships. On Peleliu in 1944, he threw his regiment in repeated bloody but ultimately futile attacks against the Umurbrogol hill mass, which ultimately led to his regiment being relieved. But through it all Puller – dehydrated, sun-scorched, and in great pain from an unhealed wound suffered in the Cape Gloucester campaign the previous year – was right up front with his men.

In the Vietnam era, leadership was still stressed as a primary virtue of Marines, but gradually the system itself foundered. The cause was a combination of problems created by the rapid expansion of the Corps, replacement and rotation policies, and drug and racial problems introduced from civilian society.

In World War II divisions had trained and fought as coherent units, often with the same leadership through several campaigns. It was a system that fostered a high degree of unit pride and cohesion. The first formations to arrive in Vietnam also came as coherent units, filled with men who had trained and served together. As the war dragged on, the rotation system developed at the end of World War II, and honed in Korea, assured that no small group would bear the full burden of the fighting. Men arrived on airliners as groups of strangers, served a 13-month tour, and departed among strangers. The really lucky ones served half their tour in the "boonies," and the balance in some relatively safe rear area. The unlucky were killed or wounded, and replaced by yet another man flowing through the replacement system. Units were chronically under strength, and the enlisted and NCO composition constantly in flux. Almost as soon as men perfected the skills that would keep them alive in combat, they went back to "the world."

The practice of rotating officers simply exacerbated the problem. Both field command and staff experience were necessary for professional advancement in a rapidly growing Corps, and in order to provide such experience officers were rotated on a regular basis. By the latter years of the war, the average tenure of a rifle battalion commander was 4½ months. Not considering temporary officers, some served as little as six weeks in their billet. The tenure of junior officers, limited not only by the inevitable casualties but also by the constant appetite of rear-area commands, was even less.

The rapid turnover, the fact that units might be in the field and separated from base areas for prolonged periods, or attached to some other command, might mean that a junior Marine served his tour without really knowing his battalion commander. It was not a matter of senior officers being "chateau generals." The vast majority of officers and senior NCOs were men of professionalism and integrity, and served in the field alongside their men. It was simply a dysfunctional system.

Communications

One of the single biggest changes in the Corps' structure since the Pacific and Korean conflicts was in tactical communications. In previous wars telephonic communications were common because the radios were bulky, operated on limited frequencies, and were often unreliable. The appearance of a truly practical, man-portable, multi-channel FM radio greatly improved communications at lower command levels, and made it feasible to place immediate-response artillery and air support assets at the disposal of small-unit commanders.

Unlike older radios, those in use in Vietnam could switch rapidly among frequencies, making possible more complex communications networks and reducing the number and bulk of radios carried by ground troops, vehicles, and command units.

The ubiquitous PRC-25 or "Prick 25" backpack radiotelephone brought about this revolution. It allowed the infantry platoon commander, or even squad leaders, to communicate with mortar sections, artillery, tanks, or aircraft

Man-portable multi-channel FM radios revolutionized combat communications. These heavily burdened men are an air control team equipped with PRC-25 radios, on Operation *Allen Brooke*, 1968. Note the large supply of smoke marker grenades, and the pack board used by the man in the background. (NARA)

controllers. Of course the enemy recognized the importance of communications, and the man with the long antenna waving over his head, and tethered to someone important by a coiled phone handset cord, was a primary target.

More powerful FM receiver/transmitters such as the RT-246/VRC with radio set AN/VRC-12, RT-524/VRC with radio set AN/VRC-46 or -47, and RT-505/PRC-25 with radio AN/VRC-53, equipped tanks and other vehicles. More powerful but bulkier AN/MRC-83, -87, -109, and –110 provided longer-ranged communications.

The ability to switch frequencies and monitor multiple frequencies provided the capability for a quick and versatile net of communications, rather than relying upon linear communications relayed through several intermediary commands. There were downsides to the revolution in communications. The very flexibility of the system increased the potential for micro-management, when higher commands could intervene directly in operations.

Telephonic communications were still used in fixed base areas, and in the artillery at battery level. These systems might operate as part of a temporary net, as in an artillery battery, or through larger systems with a central switchboard. Communications Company, 5th Communications Battalion, operated a central communications facility at Danang for coordinating radio, telephonic, and Teletype systems throughout the I Corps region. By late 1969 III MAF was tied in to several communications networks, including the AUTOVON system in Saigon, which provided direct-dial services to any location in the world.

III MAF headquarters communicated with its subordinate and superior commands primarily by encrypted Teletype, transmitted over landlines or radio.

Construction, maintenance, and operation of the complex net of communications were the responsibility of the 5th and 7th Communications battalions. Tasks included erection of telephone poles, cable laying and maintenance, and operation of central switchboards and radio relay stations.

Rapid and direct communications did not come without cost. In past wars a field command like III MAF would have reported upward through a linear chain of communications: III MAF to FMFPAC, thence to CINCPAC, to the JCS/Secretary of Defense, and thence to the President. As the Vietnam War grew into a political liability, it was increasingly common for the President and Secretary of Defense to bypass several layers of command and communicate directly with subordinate commands. The most common "jump" was from the President directly to MACV.

Heavier special-purpose radios and long-range radios were more often seen in fixed positions or vehicle mounts. These air traffic controllers are using a radio in a vehicle parked in a trench, following the destruction of the control tower at the Khe Sanh Combat Base by enemy shelling, early 1968. (MCRC)

Intelligence

Acquisition of detailed and timely intelligence data is even more critical in a counter-guerrilla war than in conventional warfare. In I Corps deep reconnaissance was the responsibility of MACV-SOG (Special Operations Group), but III MAF had its own intelligence and reconnaissance functions to provide for region-specific and immediate tactical needs. The vast majority of this intelligence and reconnaissance effort was conducted by air and ground observation, supplemented by human (HUMINT) and electronic intelligence (ELINT).

Aerial photography and remote sensing comprised most observation of enemy activities, and Marine Observation Squadrons One and Two, and Marine Composite Reconnaissance Squadron One, flew the majority of such missions. The data was collected and analyzed by III MAF G-2 Photographic Imagery Interpretation Center, and distributed to subordinate commands.

Ground reconnaissance was the responsibility of the division recon battalions, and the force reconnaissance companies. Division recon battalions were organized along the lines of infantry battalions, but without heavy weapons components. Each consisted of an H&S company and four reconnaissance companies (A through D), though at one time 3rd Reconnaissance Battalion had a Company E. Their responsibilities were immediate reconnaissance, as well as to provide waterway surveillance and security, and even to train scuba divers for bridge inspection and security.

Force recon companies were independent units intended to function at corps level. In Vietnam, the force recon companies were at times attached to – or even absorbed by – the divisional battalions. In 1969 force recon was centralized, with 1st and 3rd Force Recon companies directed by the Surveillance and Reconnaissance Center of III MAF. In addition to long-range reconnaissance, force recon patrols were primarily responsible for directing and assessing the results of artillery and air strikes (including ARC LIGHT) deep within enemy territories and base areas. These patrols also conducted field wiretaps of enemy communications, secured prisoners for interrogation, and emplaced electronic sensors.

Small observation teams from the division reconnaissance battalion and the force reconnaissance companies were a primary source of intelligence. Contrary to popular lore, the goal of these teams was to avoid detection, not to fight. (MCRC)

A typical patrol consisted of a leader (officer or senior NCO), RTO, three riflemen, and a medical corpsman. The RTO could communicate with his own command, supporting units, or tactical aircraft. An artillery battery on call, and an emergency helicopter extraction flight on standby might also support the patrol.

Several programs provided HUMINT, the most lucrative of which was probably the Chieu Hoi ("open arms") defector program. Small Interrogation Translation Teams (ITT) questioned prisoners acquired through capture or desertion. The 17th ITT scored one of the war's invaluable coups when Lieutenant La Thanh Tonc, an NVA defector, revealed the enemy's basic plan for an assault on the isolated Khe Sanh Combat Base.

Marine Counterintelligence Teams (CITs) operated local spy networks to acquire intelligence through civilian sources that might have contact with NVA or VC formations. In some cases these networks operated inside North Vietnam to monitor troop movements, and actually infiltrated NVA command units.

Many details of ELINT operations in Vietnam are still classified or restricted. First Radio Battalion conducted interception and analysis of enemy radio communications. This unit consisted of an H&S Company, and an Operations Company. The Operations Company deployed six platoons, whose task organization varied by mission, to firebases and other forward positions. Information from remote seismic, magnetic and infrared sensors emplaced by airdrop or ground patrol was broadcast to bases in Thailand, where it was analyzed and relayed to the intelligence and target information officers of Marine regiments by voice radio or teletype. Remote sensor

Prisoners, interrogated by intelligence translation teams or through interpreters in the field, were major sources of tactical and strategic information. Here a VC prisoner, at right center, has guided a tank-infantry team to a hidden bunker complex near Marble Mountain. (MCRC)

information could not be used for targeting in real time, but was used to detect units in transit to suspected base areas. Such base areas were targeted for aircraft or artillery strikes.

Morale

The collective national will to fight and accept the inevitable casualties was the single most important factor in the wars of the late 20th century. It was the absence of this will, and not the enemy's military skill, that eventually decided the conflict in Vietnam.

The war in Vietnam severely damaged the Marine Corps as an institution. The Corps that embarked upon the war in 1965 was a force of idealistic volunteers, led in large part by long-service professional officers and NCOs. By the nadir of the war in 1969–70, the combat units in Vietnam were feeling the effects of all the issues that racked the United States as a society. The late 1960s were a historical nexus where several trends coincided and fed upon each other. Growing opposition to a costly war with no apparent end in sight fueled distrust of political leadership at every level. The counterculture "hippie" movement was fueled by disengagement from society and an increasing social acceptance of drug use. Violent "black power" factions that were an unintended consequence of the civil rights movement increasingly confronted law enforcement and white society as a whole. All these problems inevitably spilled over into a military that because of broad military conscription drew its members from all sectors of society.

As the war became increasingly unpopular, and a growing sense of the futility of the struggle emerged, national and troop morale plummeted. Combat troops (especially the infantry) always tend for good reason to be cynical, and by the latter years of the war the troops often felt that they were simply being expended for no discernible reason. This impression was heightened by the relentless grinding combat and heavy losses suffered in the fighting against the NVA. In the Marine Corps disillusionment was expressed not only in the fatalism and alcohol abuse familiar from prior wars, but in record levels of disciplinary infractions and drug use.

Since earliest recorded history, alcohol has been the fighting man's drug of choice to anesthetize the mind. Alcohol abuse probably reached its global peak in late World War II. In the Vietnam era, drug use (particularly marijuana) in Western societies often held less of a social stigma than drunkenness. Other drugs, notably heroin, were also readily available in Vietnam. A 1972 report indicated that 48 percent of Marines had reported using drugs at some time, and that 32 percent were "regular users."

Despite these problems Marine forces in Vietnam suffered a far less severe collapse of unit integrity and combat efficiency than did their Army counterparts. While rates of desertion, AWOL, and drug use were marginally higher than those of Army units, the incidence of practices indicative of a severe loss of unit cohesion – fragging (assassination of leaders) and outright mutiny – were profoundly less. There were probably several institutional reasons for these differences.

Despite their cynicism, individual Marines still considered themselves members of an elite. Though they would freely engage in systematic self-pitying "griping," individual Marines still functioned aggressively in very intense combat to maintain individual and unit pride, and to support their friends. The bitter and fatalistic attitude might seem bizarre to a rational person outside the group: "I know you're just using me up as cannon fodder. But I'm still me, and I'm tough as hell. So do your worst."

Aggressive intervention by NCOs ensured that problem drug abusers and malcontents did not "infect" larger groups. By virtue of its smaller size and reputation as an elite combat force, the Corps was also able to be much more selective in its choice of officers and NCOs. The common theme was that the

Table of morale

	USMC	US Army
Desertion rate	37/1,000	36/1,000
Increase vs. pre-war	205%	277%
AWOL rate	141/1,000	103/1,000
Drug use	32%	28%
Fragging incidents	121[1]	1,016[2]
Mutiny incidents	26[1]	245[3]

Notes:
1 1964–72.
2 1965–72.
3 One division alone, 1970.
Source: MAJ Richard A. Gabriel, "Professionalism Versus Managerialism in Vietnam,"
Air University Review, 1981

Corps was able to function even in a period of severe adversity because it emphasized old-fashioned discipline and military leadership, as opposed to the organizational "military management" principles then in vogue.

With the advent of the "black power" movement, racial issues also became a major cause of disruption that at times resulted in fights and a few outright riots between factions divided along racial lines. As with most morale problems, such conflicts were typically limited to rear areas, or occurred when troops were otherwise unoccupied. In combat racial conflicts subsided or disappeared entirely.

Combat operations

The war in Vietnam necessitated far different tactical operations than the fighting in the Pacific War or the Korean conflict. In Vietnam terrain and physical objectives were unimportant except as a location to fix and destroy the enemy, but the enemy frequently retained the ability to slip away rather than be destroyed. In the I Corps region, the Marines actually fought two wars. The conflict in the immediate area of the DMZ was defensive and almost conventional. Heavy NVA artillery firing from positions across the border pounded Marine positions. The thinly spread American and South Vietnamese defenses were subject to constant ground attack, and sometimes placed under outright siege, most famously at the Khe Sanh Combat Base in 1968. The Marines relied upon aggressive patrolling by large and small units to close the gaps between strong points and deny passage to the enemy.

Farther south, the war against the VC – and the larger NVA units that appeared as the war wore on – was one to separate the people from the guerrillas. It was an endless campaign of squad-scale battles of patrols and ambushes, punctuated by sweeps.

During the course of the war the Marines conducted 195 named operations, beginning with *Blastout I* on 2–3 August 1965, a search and clear operation conducted by elements of 1/3 and 1/9. *Blastout I* provided an iconic image of the war when the village of Cam Ne, from which the Marines of D/1/9 had been fired upon, was ordered burned. A CBS film crew recorded the destruction.

The last true operation was *Scott Orchard*, the search for an alleged POW camp in NVA Base Area 112, Quang Nam province. The final gasp of the war was Operation *Frequent Wind*, the evacuation of Saigon in late April 1975.

Starlite: a typical sweep operation

Operation *Starlite* was the first large sweep operation, typical in its complexity, and established the pattern for the remainder of the war. (The operation was supposed to have been *Satellite*, but a harried clerk working by dim lantern light mistyped several forms, and Operation *Satellite* became *Starlite*.)

Starlite involved two rifle battalions (one each from the 3rd and 4th Marines) and all supporting arms, helicopter and sea-borne forces, and cooperation from US Army and South Vietnamese units. The operation was under the command of Colonel Oscar Peatross, commanding officer of the 7th Marines. Since 3/7 was to be the operational reserve, it included both III MAF and SLF units; a delay in launching the operation was caused by the necessity to move the SLF from the Philippines.

Combat in Vietnam was always chaotic, and *Starlite* was very typical in the way that opposing forces stumbled upon each other, small units became disoriented in the complex terrain, and coordination broke down. The following very simplified account is told from the viewpoint of the Marines, but it must have been even more confusing for the Communist force, with less capable communications, and confronted by an enemy that seized the initiative through mobility and kept appearing in unexpected places.

On 6 August 1965, 3rd Marine Division received orders to attack the 1st VC Regiment (60th and 80th Bns, 52nd Company, and 45th Weapons Bn) consisting of some 1,500 men. This force was reported by a deserter to be assembling in the Van Truong village, in preparation for an attack on the Marine base at Chu Lai, 12km to the north. On 17 August M/3/3 moved into the area mounted in LVTP-5s, then inland on foot to establish blocking positions northwest of the objective. The next morning at 0615 hours, the 155mm howitzers of Kilo Battery, 4/12 opened preparatory fires on isolated landing zones (LZs) RED, WHITE, and BLUE. Marine A-4 and F-4 jets pounded the LZs and GREEN Beach with bombs, napalm, and cannon fire. At 0630 companies I and K, with Company L 3/3 in reserve, supported by three M67 flame tanks and five M48A3 gun tanks, landed at GREEN Beach and moved

Command list, Operation Starlite	
7th Marines (operational control)	Col. Oscar F. Peatross
3rd Bn, 7th Marines (operational reserve)	Lt. Col. Thomas H. Bodley
3rd Bn, 3rd Marines	Lt. Col. Joseph E. Muir
3rd Bn, 3rd Marines	Maj. Andrew G. Comer[1]
2nd Bn, 4th Marines	Lt. Col. Joseph R. Fisher
1 Placed in command of hasty relief force to rescue ambushed armored column.	

Operation Starlite, 17–19 August 1965.

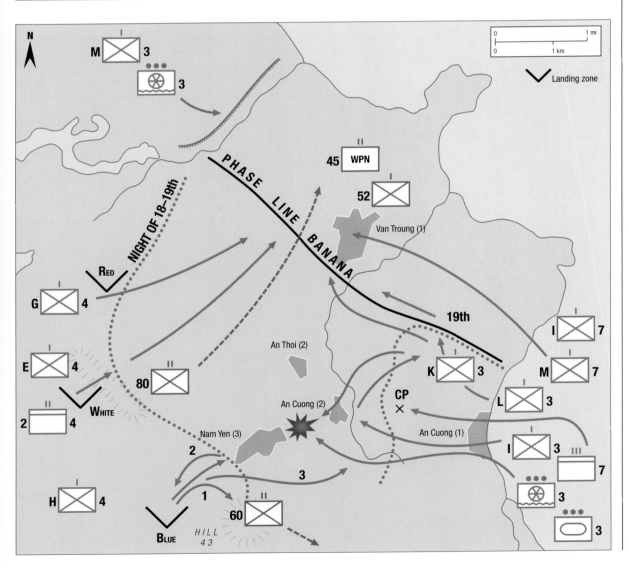

quickly inland. At 0645 troop-carrying helicopters deposited Company G, 2/4, in LZ RED, and at 0730 Company E landed at LZ WHITE and Company H, 2/4, at LZ BLUE. Operational headquarters was established just inland from GREEN Beach.

K/3/3 moved quickly inland until they met enemy resistance at phase line BANANA, a prominent ridgeline about 2km inland. The concept of phase lines was introduced in the fighting on Pacific islands in World War II. In poorly mapped or confusing terrain, attacking units would pause on easily recognizable terrain features while adjacent units – which might be moving more slowly or meeting heavier resistance – came back into alignment. This helped prevent units from accidentally engaging each other or calling down artillery fire on friendly troops, and minimized the occurrence of exposed flanks that the enemy could exploit either to counterattack or to slip away.

Stiff resistance near BANANA necessitated commitment of the operational reserve, L/3/3, but by nightfall the Marines occupied the ridge. Company E met resistance as soon as it left LZ WHITE, and expended several hours in squad- and platoon-scale assaults to clear a ridgeline.

LZ BLUE sat in a maze of rice paddies situated among small hills and three hamlets. When Company H landed they came down smack atop the 60th VC Battalion. The surprised enemy failed to react immediately, but heavy machine gun fire from Hill 43 raked the following helicopters. Platoons dispatched toward the hill and the nearby hamlet, Nam Yen 3, were driven back, so the company commander called in air strikes, and concentrated his force against the hill. The assault drove the enemy off the hill in fierce fighting. India/3/3, moving inland from the beach, was granted permission to cross the battalion boundary and attack An Cuong 2. The hamlet proved to be a VC fortified position, with trench lines, tunnel complexes, and numerous heavy-weapons positions. After a confused fight in which the company commander was killed, India Company secured the hamlet.

Tanks, infantry, and older UH-34 helicopters of the Special Landing Force come together in the opening phases of Operation *Starlite*, 1965. In its complexity and use of components from multiple commands, it set the pattern for future sweep operations. (NARA)

At about this time the command post dispatched a supply column – five LVTP-5s escorted by three tanks – toward An Cuong 2. Company I moved off toward BANANA to help Company K, leaving two squads behind to guard a crippled helicopter. At about the same time H/2/4 moved toward An Cuong 2 to link up with I/3/3. In the confusion, the company commander thought that India had cleared the hamlet of Nam Yen 3. Enemy entrenched in that hamlet brought Company H under heavy fire, driving them back toward LZ BLUE at mid-afternoon. The arrival of medical evacuation helicopters disrupted the company's march, and in the confusion one platoon became separated and pinned down, but was rescued by the efforts of the two squads left behind by I/3/3. These orphans joined forces and sought refuge in the direction of An Cuong 2. The other two platoons of H/2/4 were ordered back to LZ BLUE to dig in and await reinforcement.

Meanwhile the supply column had become disoriented in the thick woods, and was ambushed between An Cuong 2 and Nam Yen 3. To make matters even worse, a panicked radio operator kept his transmit button on, preventing anyone else from broadcasting on the frequency. Nobody knew where the trapped vehicles were.

The relief force organized to help H/2/4 – the worn-out India Company, a hastily assembled group of headquarters personnel, and the one remaining gun tank, under command of Major Andrew Comer, 3/3's executive officer – was diverted to search for the supply column. Near Hill 30 this group ran into strong resistance. The tank was disabled and the headquarters detachment driven to ground in some rice paddies. India Company pressed on through An Cuong 2, only to be pinned in place before they could reach the trapped vehicles. The wandering orphans joined up with India Company.

Colonel Peatross called up Lima/3/7 from the operational reserve. This unit also encountered heavy resistance east of An Cuong 2, but drove the VC back and forced them to break contact. The efforts of the two infantry companies relieved the pressure on the trapped supply column. Rather than press on in the darkness and confusion, the two infantry companies pulled back, and the supply column, no longer under attack, remained in place.

During the night Colonel Peatross adjusted the original plan, and units were reassigned. Company H, 2/4 and Major Comer's bloodied composite group were withdrawn to reserve positions near the Command Post. The remaining reserve companies, India and Mike, 3/7, came ashore.

At 0730 on 19 August companies K and L, 3/3, resumed the advance toward Van Truong 1, the original objective, while E and G, 2/4, moved eastward to meet them. Both units pressed the VC against blocking positions held by M/3/3 on the north, and I and M, 3/7, on the south. The VC fought tenaciously from bunkers, trenches and caves. Marine units frequently had to reverse direction and attack positions in areas thought already cleared. By 0900 companies I and M, 3/7, entered An Cuong 2, and also relieved the survivors of the supply column, which had suffered 60 percent casualties. By 1030 the two major forces had linked up and continued to advance on a broad front against dwindling VC resistance.

The next day 2/4 and 3/3 were withdrawn, replaced by 1/7 and units of the 2nd ARVN Division. *Starlite* continued for five more days as patrols swept through the area rooting out enemy survivors and destroying any positions or supplies they found. The VC forces suffered 614 known dead (560 in the first three days of heavy fighting), nine captured, and an unknown number of wounded. The Marines suffered 45 dead and 203 wounded.

For both sides it was typical of the operations that would drag on for the next seven years. The Marines had descended upon an area occupied by Communist forces, precipitating a protracted and savage battle. The Marines had inflicted disproportionately heavy casualties and controlled the battlefield, but the Communist forces had fought skillfully and survived to fight another day. It was a war of attrition, but also of endurance and will.

Pipestone Canyon: the cordon of Tay Bang An

The isolation and probable destruction of a VC sapper company in the abandoned village of Tay Bang An in July 1969 is an example of the advantages that air mobility provided. It also illustrates the difficulty of pinning the VC in place, and the frustration of limited observable results.

Intelligence reports and air observation convinced the commander of the 1st Marines that the village served as a base and staging area, and he received permission to launch a hasty battalion-scale cordon and sweep. At 0800 on the morning of 15 July CH-46 helicopters carrying the reinforced 2/1 (three of the battalion's line companies, plus D Company, 1st Battalion) under Lt Col Harold G. Glasgow approached landing zones on four sides of the fortified base area. All the helicopters came under heavy small-arms fire, with one seriously damaged and forced to divert to an emergency landing along Highway 1 to the southeast. Two landing zones had to be shifted because of the heavy fire, delaying the operation by an hour. Once on the

Tay Bang An, 15 July 1969.

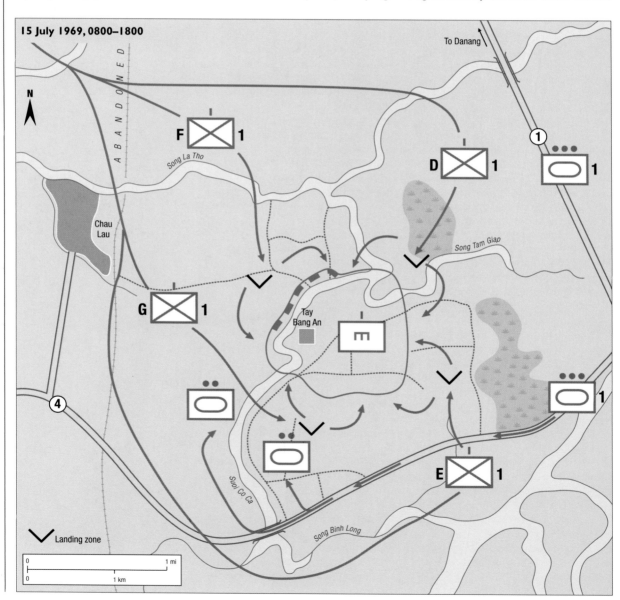

ground the four companies fanned out to enclose the abandoned village. Company F met the heaviest resistance, taking heavy machine gun and RPG fire from bunkers along the north bank of the Soui Co Ca. The company pushed through the bunkers, driving the enemy across the stream and finding four bodies.

Through the remainder of the day the Marines established a defensive line around the enemy positions, emplacing mortars and machine guns. In the afternoon a platoon of tanks moved down Highway 1, west along Highway 4, and joined the defense along the southwestern side of the perimeter.

All day on 16 July the Marines tightened the cordon, slowly pushing forward. The trapped VC probed at various points, seeking a weak spot in the cordon, and then launched a breakout attempt along the south bank of the Soui Co Ca, a sector defended by G Company and a section of tanks. Though the attack penetrated Marine positions, the attempt ultimately failed as an organized escape.

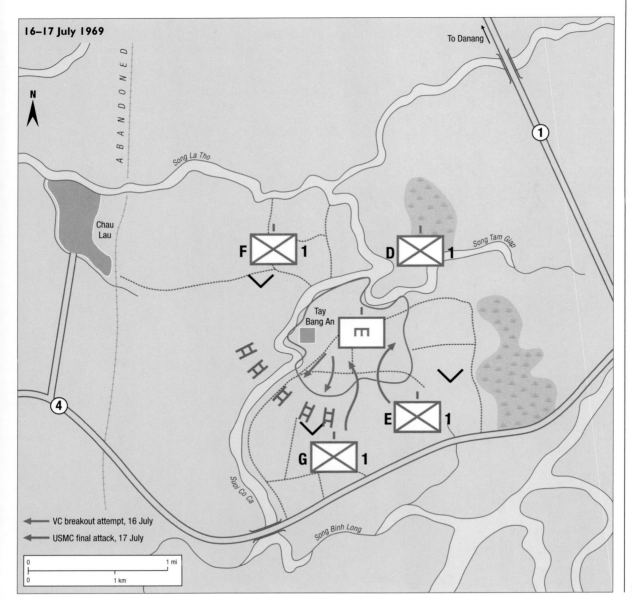

On the morning of 17 July, the infantry companies along the south perimeter penetrated into the village and initiated a series of searches. Late in the day the operation was secured, and the battalion boarded helicopters for the return to their base.

Aerial observation before the operation had reported a minimum of 50 enemy observed in the open at one time, with undoubtedly far more under concealment, the battalion counted only 20 enemy dead, and captured 14. (Marine casualties in this small sub-operation are not itemized separately from the larger *Pipestone Canyon*.) The still unanswered questions are several. Was the estimate of enemy strength reliable? The volume of fire directed against the helicopters seems to indicate a large number of defenders. Did the bulk of the enemy somehow escape or go to ground to avoid detection? Or did the VC hide many of their casualties, a standard practice?

Dewey Canyon: assault on NVA Base Area 611

Dewey Canyon and its preliminaries are an example of the large, almost conventional offensives directed against NVA base areas along the remote Vietnam–Laos border at the height of the war. The initial phase consisted of a series of leapfrog air landings to secure an approach to the potential battle area, followed by a regimental offensive with the goal of destroying enemy forces and matériel, and severing his logistics routes.[5]

In early 1969 it was obvious from aerial reconnaissance and enemy anti-aircraft fire that the NVA was developing a major logistics route into South

In the more conventional war against NVA base areas, helicopters airlifted engineer equipment to construct firebases, and then airlifted artillery into position to protect the advance of the infantry through rugged and trackless terrain. These guns are at Fire Support Base Cunningham during Operation *Dewey Canyon*, 1969. (MCRC)

5 For an infantryman's view of this operation, see Osprey Warrior No. 23: *US Marine In Vietnam 1965–73*.

Vietnam by repairing an abandoned road that entered from Laos south of the Song Da Krong (river) Valley. Identified units included the 6th and 9th NVA regiments, 65th Artillery Regiment (with 122mm guns, and anti-aircraft guns up to 37mm), and 83rd Engineer Regiment. The terrain that would have to be traversed to attack this route comprised roadless, forested mountains. Northwest trending ridges rise up for hundreds of meters above the rocky valley floors, and slopes are often up to 75 degrees or even vertical cliffs. Heavy rain frequently turns the thin soil into slimy mud.

An overland attack would be impossibly slow, and the powerful enemy air defense imposed unacceptable risks for a direct airmobile assault. The final operational plan called for heliborne assaults to establish a series of fire support bases (FSBs), staging from the large Vandegrift Combat Base. Artillery airlifted into each FSB in succession would allow the next landing to proceed under the protection of friendly artillery. Finally, an air-supplied forward logistics base would allow infantry to advance into the enemy base area in a conventional broad-front attack.

Beginning with Phase I, infantry and artillery reoccupied abandoned FSBs Henderson and Tun Tavern on 18 and 20 January. After shelling FSB Shiloh from FSB Henderson, it was reoccupied on 21 January. On 22 January four companies of 2nd Battalion, 9th Marines seized landing zones RAZOR and DALLAS, and with the support of helicopter-transported light engineer bulldozers, began construction of FSB facilities. By 24 January FSB Razor supported the 9th Marines' headquarters, the 12th Marines' headquarters and

Command list, Operation *Dewey Canyon*	
3rd Marine Division	Maj. Gen, Raymond G. Davis
9th Marines	Col. Robert H. Barrow
1st Bn, 9th Marines	Lt. Col. George W. Smith
2nd Bn, 9th Marines	Lt. Col. George C. Fox
3rd Bn, 9th Marines	Lt. Col. Elliott R. Lane
12th Marines	Col. Peter J. Mulroney
2nd Bn, 12th Marines	Lt. Col. Joseph R. Scopp

Casualties	USMC	NVA
KIA	130	1,617
WIA	920	unknown
Captured	0	5

Material captured/destroyed	USMC	NVA
Artillery[1]	0	16
AA guns	0	73
mortars	0	26
machine guns	0	104
trucks	0	92
tracked vehicles	0	1
food (tons)	0	110
ammunition (rounds)	0	807,000

1 Does not include damaged/returned to service.

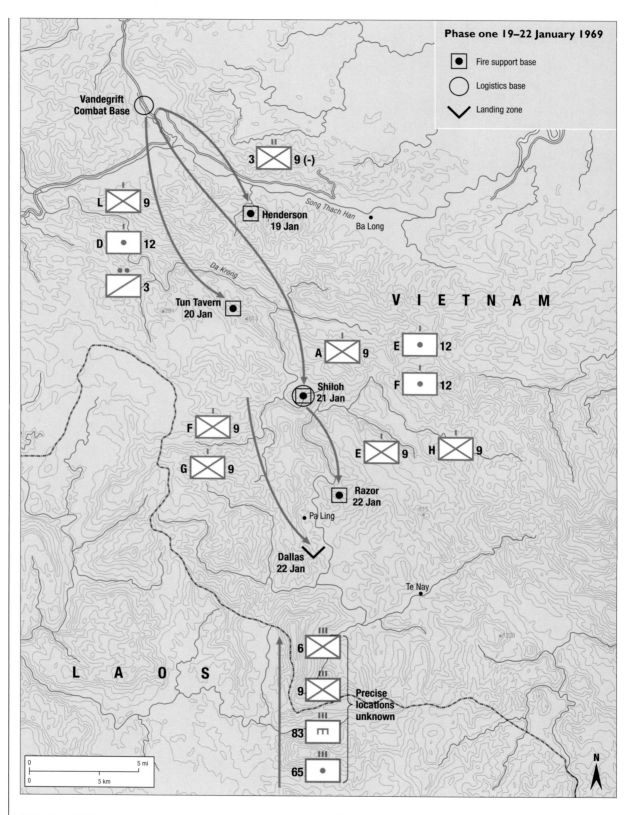

Phase one 19–22 January 1969

- ◉ Fire support base
- ○ Logistics base
- ⋁ Landing zone

Vandegrift Combat Base

3 ⊠ 9 (-)

L ⊠ 9

D ⊡ 12

⊠ 3

Tun Tavern 20 Jan ◉

Henderson 19 Jan ◉

Song Thach Han

Ba Long

Da Krong

V I E T N A M

A ⊠ 9

E ⊡ 12

F ⊡ 12

Shiloh 21 Jan ◉

F ⊠ 9

G ⊠ 9

E ⊠ 9   H ⊠ 9

Razor 22 Jan ◉

Pa Ling

Dallas 22 Jan ⋁

Te Nay

L A O S

6 ⊠

9 ⊠

Precise locations unknown

83 ⊓

65 ⊡

N

0 ____ 5 mi
0 ____ 5 km

ABOVE AND OPPOSITE The opening phase of Operation *Dewey Canyon*, 19–28 January 1969 (see also pp.90–91).

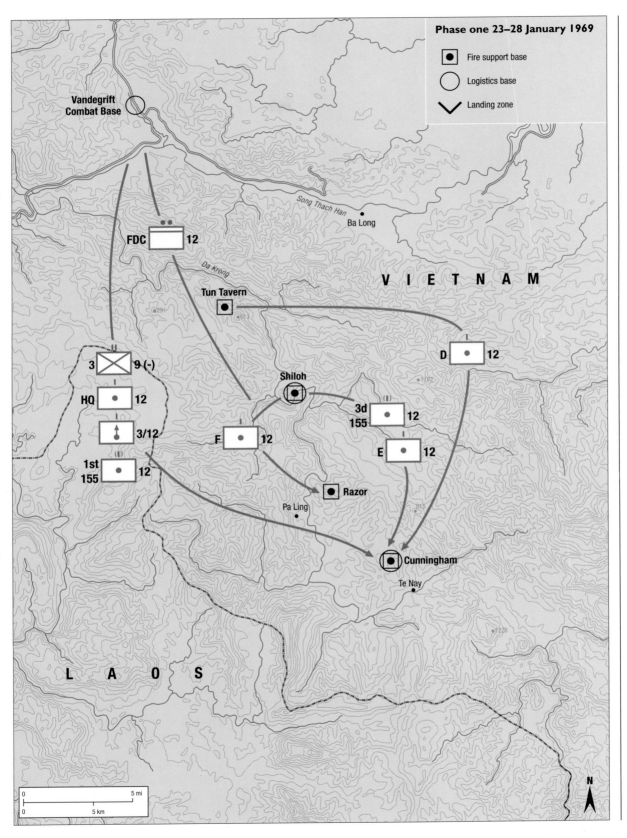

Phase one 23–28 January 1969

- ▣ Fire support base
- ◯ Logistics base
- ﹀ Landing zone

Vandegrift Combat Base

Song Thach Han

Ba Long

FDC 12

Da Krong

Tun Tavern

V I E T N A M

D 12

Shiloh

3 9 (-)

3d 12
155

HQ 12

F 12

E 12

3/12

1st 12
155

Razor

Pa Ling

Cunningham

Te Nay

L A O S

0 ——— 5 mi
0 ——— 5 km

N

87

Fire Direction Center, a battery of 105mm howitzers, and a logistics center. 1,544 Marines and 46 tons of cargo had been airlifted in.

On 25 January 3rd Battalion, 9th Marines helicopered onto a ridgeline above the Da Krong Valley, and began construction of FSB Cunningham. By 29 January the base hosted: 9th Marines headquarters; batteries D and E (105mm), Mortar Battery 2nd Battalion, and the 1st and 3rd Provisional 155mm batteries of the 12th Marines; and a logistics unit capable of supporting eight rifle companies.

During Phase II the 9th Marines consolidated their hold on the areas north of the river, patrolling the areas around the new bases, tapping into an NVA telephone trunk line, and discovering the abandoned NVA 88th Field Hospital (these facilities were often set up near reliable water sources). F Company constructed FSB Erskine, and K Company secured an LZ and began construction of FSB Lightning, immediately occupied by ARVN infantry and artillery units.

On 31 January G Company moved out from LZ DALLAS toward the huge Co Ka Leuye hill mass. Nine days of bad weather allowed enemy 122mm guns – normally kept inactive by aerial observation – to shell Cunningham, disabling a 155mm howitzer and destroying the 3rd Provisional 155mm Battery's FDC. All infantry companies were ordered to pull back into defensive positions. Unable to receive re-supply by air, G Company began to withdraw toward DALLAS on 4 February, only to stumble into a major ambush. After a four-day struggle with the enemy, weather, and terrain, the company linked up with E Company at DALLAS.

Phase III commenced on 11 February when the 3rd Battalion crossed the Song Da Krong, followed the next day by the other two battalions. Each battalion was to push along parallel ridges with two companies moving in tandem along each ridgeline. The NVA resisted desperately, using suicide tactics and running company-scale battles to slow the Marine advance. In the early morning hours of 17 February a platoon of suicide sappers supported by a reinforced infantry company broke into FSB Cunningham, disabling one howitzer and the FDC before they were annihilated.

In heavy fighting on the 18th through 20th, the 1st Battalion penetrated bunker lines, capturing trucks, a five-ton artillery tractor, and two Soviet-made 122mm guns. By 20 February elements of the 2nd Battalion were watching NVA traffic withdrawing to the west along Route 922. Although artillery fire was called down, the tenuous political situation – peace negotiations were underway in Paris – blocked approval to cross the border and interdict the road.

On 21 February Hotel Company was ordered to set up an ambush along the road, half a kilometer inside Laos, but to be back across the border by 0630 the next morning. There was some question about whether this incursion was authorized. As the company ambushed an NVA truck column, 3rd Division headquarters monitoring radio traffic recommended not notifying MACV until the rules of engagement had been clarified. Presented with a *fait accompli*, on 24 February General Creighton Abrams (MACV) approved the incursion into Laos, but attempted to limit the news of the action.

In intense fighting that lasted until 1 March, the Marines inflicted heavy casualties, and captured the largest enemy arms cache of the war, tons of food, heavy maintenance equipment, construction equipment, a fuel depot, 122mm guns and 37mm anti-aircraft guns. The primary accomplishment, however, was to disrupt the NVA's logistical base for conducting combat operations in the populous regions to the east.

On 3 March the Marine infantry in Laos was transported by helicopter back to Vandegrift. For political reasons, all casualties were listed as incurred "near Quang Tri Province, South Vietnam."

In its last gasp *Dewey Canyon* typified all the savagery, frustration, and political ambiguity of the entire Vietnam experience.

The Struggle for Binh Ngiah: CAP in Action

In early 1966 the VC ruled Binh Ngiah, a cluster of seven hamlets spread along the northwest bank of the strategic Tra Bong River. The marshes of the southeast bank were undisputed VC territory. The men of the small Popular Forces detachment, driven from their homes, established an outpost on a nearby hill, from which they launched occasional sorties to harass the VC.

At the request of a local police officer, on 10 June a twelve-man CAP squad selected from over 100 volunteers moved into an abandoned villa west of the village. The Marines and PFs fortified the mansion with a high bamboo fence to detonate RPG rockets, a moat, and a barrier of sharpened stakes.

By late July the Marines and PFs owned the night, ambushing VC patrols, driving out the tax collectors, and shooting up transport boats on the river; unknown to the Marines, they had established themselves athwart a major VC supply route. The cost was high, including the assassination of the police officer in his mother's house, and the death of one Marine. In early September Communist reinforcements arrived to put an end to the CAP detachment, and there were numerous contacts with NVA patrols.

On the cold, rainy night of 14 September a PF patrol sent into the village to screen the rear of the small base, called Fort Page after the dead Marine, instead sheltered in local homes. Two other patrols of Marines and PFs were abroad, leaving six Marines, ten PFs, and two local policemen to defend the fort. The home also hosted about a dozen unarmed civilian village leaders.

Just after midnight, 80 VC of the P31 District Force Company, 60 men of 5 Company, NVA 409 Battalion, and a squad of special sappers attacked the unprotected rear of Fort Page. Five Marines, including the squad leader, and six PFs died in the initial onslaught and the fighting inside the compound. Flares that would have summoned back the patrols were invisible in the rain; one patrol heard the fighting but was pinned down by the VC outside the walls. The PF medic, believing all was lost, buried the last unconscious Marine in the garbage pit, but he dug his way out to help the PFs in their final defense. The defenders had six rounds left when the attackers retreated, scattering propaganda leaflets in their wake.

The Commanding General of the 1st Marine Division gave the survivors a choice to depart, but all chose to stay in their village. Two nights later, led by a new sergeant who had volunteered from a hospital bed, the Marines and PFs ambushed a VC patrol in the village, killing the Executive Officer of the P31 Company and 15 others. For the remainder of the night the CAP detachment waited in the darkness. Dawn revealed to the villagers only watchful Marines and PFs, and dead VC, silent evidence that despite the boastful propaganda leaflets, the CAP still ruled Binh Ngiah. They would do so for another 14 months, until relieved.

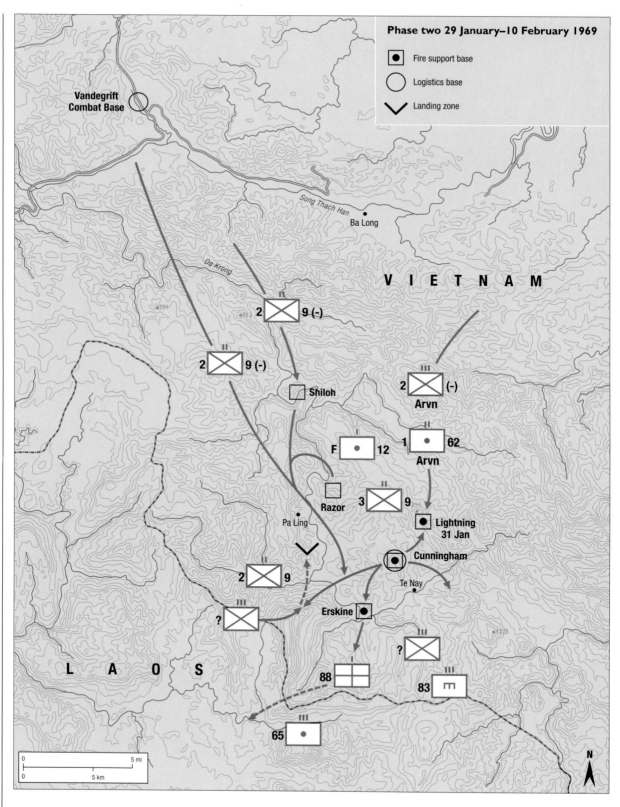

Vandegrift
Combat Base

Song Thach Han

Ba Long

Da Krong

V I E T N A M

291

673

2 ⊠ 9 (-)

2 ⊠ 9 (-)

2 ⊠ (-)
Arvn

⬜ Shiloh

F ⊡ 12

1 ⊡ 62
Arvn

⬜ Razor

3 ⊠ 9

815

Pa Ling

∨

⊡ Lightning
31 Jan

2 ⊠ 9

◉ Cunningham

Te Nay

Erskine ⊡

1228

? ⊠

? ⊠

⊞ 88

⊞ 83

65 ⊡

0 ————— 5 mi

0 ————— 5 km

L A O S

N ⬆

Above and opposite Operation *Dewey Canyon*, 29 January–1 March 1969.

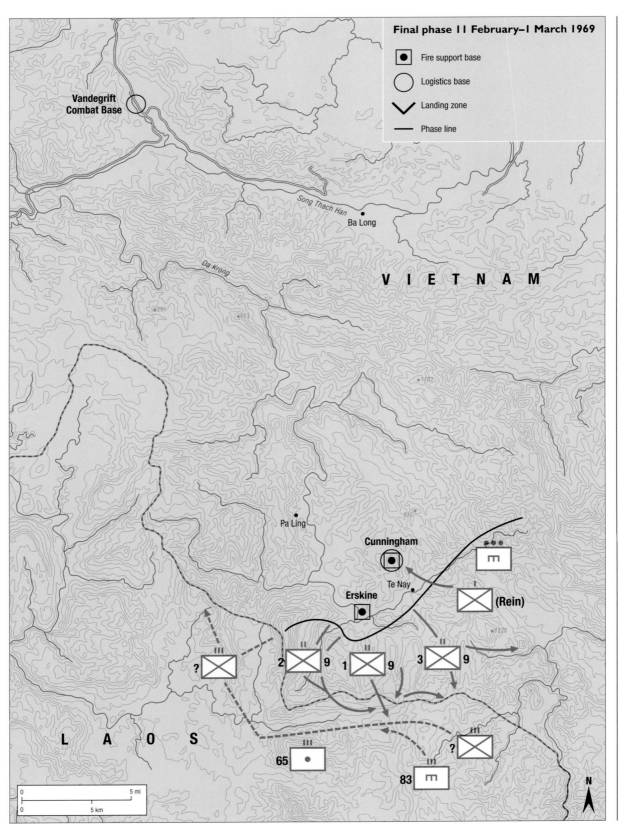

Final phase 11 February–1 March 1969

- ⬛● Fire support base
- ◯ Logistics base
- ⋁ Landing zone
- — Phase line

Vandegrift Combat Base

Song Thach Han

Ba Long

Da Krong

V I E T N A M

Pa Ling

Cunningham

Te Nay

Erskine

(Rein)

2 ⊠ 9

1 ⊠ 9

3 ⊠ 9

? ⊠

L A O S

65 ⬛●

83 ⬛

0   5 mi
0   5 km

N

Lessons learned

The Corps' longest war proved costly to the organization in terms of more than casualties and frustration. Though some doctrines were proven sound, and the experience led to remediation of some nagging problems, the cost in institutional morale was immense.

Post World War II changes in the centerpiece of the Marines' doctrine, amphibious assault, was not tested on a large scale but overall the doctrine proved sound. Subsequent changes in high-level command structures simplified and remedied many of the confused command structure that bedeviled the Special Landing Forces. The Marine landing force commander could – if necessary – appeal to higher command levels to facilitate assumption of full command once ashore. The primary problem was with equipment, the antiquated LVTP-5 series vehicles. A replacement vehicle, the LVTP-7 series, was faster in water, better armed and protected, and was far more reliable in prolonged land operations. This vehicle, with several upgrades, still serves 30 years later.

The corollary doctrine of vertical envelopment was tested and proven sound, though the Corps' version remains less familiar than the more widely publicized Army air assault doctrine. Modern helicopter-borne Marine forces have benefited from the development of more capable helicopters, and artillery and light armored vehicles that can be airlifted by heavy helicopters. The Marines' long-awaited high-speed, over-the-horizon transport aircraft, the V-22 Osprey, remains an unrealized dream.

The all-arms doctrine proved generally sound, but the almost universal use of tanks in penny-packets for infantry support further retarded the development of a sound Marine armor doctrine. This aggravated the difficulties of procuring upgraded tanks like the M1 series, and resulted in the frantic rush to re-equip Marine tank units on the eve of the 1991 Gulf War.

Application of the Marines' *Small Wars* counterinsurgency doctrine was aborted just as it was bearing fruit in Vietnam, and was never fully tested. Subsequent analysis indicated that the fundamental doctrine was sound, and in modified form it remains a part of the Marines' diverse mission.

Perhaps the single greatest advance was in the field of logistics, long a Marine weakness. The experience gained with Force Logistics Command – in which many future high-ranking generals served – led to greater capability and flexibility at all levels of command.

All these, however, were at first outweighed by the damage done to institutional morale. The short-term problems in discipline, recruiting, and national confidence in the Marine Corps as an institution probably came as close to wrecking the Corps as any experience in its history. In the aftermath of the war, leadership returned to a hard line toward recruiting and retention, emphasizing quality of troops at the expense of quantity, and adopting what would today be termed a zero-tolerance policy with regard to substance abuse. This bore fruit only at the end of the decade-long struggle to restore the Corps to its pre-Vietnam standing.

Another long-term result of the war and the reduction of military budgets was the long delay in procurement of new equipment at all levels. Even today the Corps still struggles to modernize its equipment. Budgetary issues created significant delays in upgrading tanks, fixed-wing aircraft and artillery. Today the Corps still has not fielded replacements for its aging amphibian tractor and helicopter fleets.

All in all, Vietnam was a war the Corps would in retrospect have preferred not to fight, at least not under the terms imposed upon it by higher levels of military and civilian leadership.

Bibliography and further reading

Cosmas, Graham A. and Murray, Terrence P., *US Marines In Vietnam: Vietnamization and Redeployment, 1970–1971* (Washington DC, History and Museums Division, US Marine Corps, 1986)

Leatherneck Association, *Guidebook for Marines* (Washington, DC, Leatherneck Association, 1967 Edition)

Melson, Charles D. and Arnold, Curtis G., *US Marines In Vietnam: The War That Would Not End, 1971–1973* (Washington DC, History and Museums Division, US Marine Corps, 1991)

Melson, Charles D. and Bujeiro, Ramiro, *US Marine in Vietnam 1965–73* (London, Osprey Publishing, 1998)

Millett, Allan R., *Semper Fidelis: A History of the United States Marine Corps* (New York, NY, MacMillan Publishing, 1980)

Shumlinson, Jack and Johns, Charles M., *US Marines In Vietnam: The Landing and Buildup, 1965* (Washington DC, History and Museums Division, US Marine Corps, 1978)

Shumlinson, Jack, *US Marines In Vietnam: An Expanding War, 1966* (Washington DC, History and Museums Division, US Marine Corps, 1982)

Shumlinson, Jack, *US Marines In Vietnam: The Defining Year, 1968* (Washington DC, History and Museums Division, US Marine Corps, 1997)

Sigler, David Burns, *Vietnam Battle Chronology: US Army and Marine Corps Combat Operations, 1965–73* (Jefferson, North Carolina, MacFarland and Company, 1992)

Smith, Charles R., *US Marines In Vietnam: High Mobility and Standdown, 1969* (Washington DC, History and Museums Division, US Marine Corps, 1988)

Telfer, Gary L., Rogers, Lane and Fleming, V. Keith, *US Marines In Vietnam: Fighting the North Vietnamese, 1967* (Washington DC, History and Museums Division, US Marine Corps, 1984)

US Marine Corps, *FMF Manual 4-1, Logistical and Personnel Support* (Washington, DC, US Government Printing Office, 1970 Edition)

US Marine Corps, *FMF Manual 6-1, The Division* (Washington, DC, US Government Printing Office, 1969 Edition)

US Marine Corps, *FMF Manual 6-2, Marine Infantry Regiment* (Washington, DC, US Government Printing Office, 1966 Edition)

US Marine Corps, *FMF Manual 6-3, Marine Infantry Battalion* (Washington, DC, US Government Printing Office, 1978 Edition)

US Marine Corps, *FMF Manual 6-4, Marine Rifle Company/Platoon* (Washington, DC, US Government Printing Office, 1978 Edition)

US Marine Corps, *FMF Manual 7-1, Field Artillery Support* (Washington, DC, US Government Printing Office, 1970 Edition)

West, F.J. Jr, *Small Unit Action in Vietnam* (Washington DC, History and Museums Division, US Marine Corps, 1967)

West, F.J. Jr, *The Village* (New York, Harper and Row, 1972)

Whitlow, Robert H., *US Marines In Vietnam: The Advisory and Combat Assistance Era, 1954–1964* (Washington DC, History and Museums Division, US Marine Corps, 1977)

Additional resources include weekly Status of Forces reports filed at the USMC History and Museums Branch, Quantico, Virginia, and the collected unit diaries available on compact disc form also available through History and Museums Branch.

Abbreviations and measurements

AAA	Antiaircraft artillery	ITR	Infantry Training Regiment
ANGLICO	Air-Naval Gunfire Liaison Company	ITT	Interrogation Translation Team
ARVN	Army of the Republic of Vietnam	LAAM	Light Antiaircraft Missile
AWOL	Absent without leave	LSU	Logistical Support Unit
BLT	Battalion Landing Team	LZ	landing zone
CACO	Combined Action Company	MACV	Military Assistance Command Vietnam
CAP	Combined Action Program/Platoon	MAF	Marine Amphibious Force
CATF	Commander, Amphibious Task Forces	MAG	Marine Air Group
CG	Commanding General	MEB	Marine Expeditionary Brigade
CIT	Counterintelligence Teams	MEF	Marine Expeditionary Force
CO	Commanding officer	MEU	Marine Expeditionary Unit
COFRAM	Controlled Fragmentation Munitions	MOS	Military Occupation Specialty
COMPHIBFOR-SEVENTHFLT	Commander Amphibious Forces Seventh Fleet	MP	Military Police
		MT	Motor Transport
COMSEVENTHFLT	Commander Seventh Fleet	NCO	Non-commissioned officer
CTG (-) ARG	Commander of Task Group Amphibious Ready Group (Navy ships)	NVA	North Vietnamese Army
		PETN	Pentaerythritoltetranitrate (explosive)
CTG (-) SLF	Commander of Task Group Special Landing Force (USMC)	PF	Popular Forces
		PFC	Private First Class
DMZ	Demilitarized zone	R&R	Rest and recreation
ELINT	electronic intelligence	RF	Regional Forces
FAG	Field Artillery Group	RLT	Regimental Landing Team
FLC	Force Logistics Command	RPG	Rocket Propelled Grenade
FLS	Force Logistics Support	RTO	Radiotelephone operator
FMF	Fleet Marine Force	SLF	Special Landing Force
FMFPAC	Fleet Marine Forces Pacific	SOG	Special Operations Group
FSB	fire support base	SP	Self-propelled
FSR	Force Service Regiment	SPLT	Shore Party Liaison Teams
H&I	Harassment and Interdiction	STRAC	Strategic Army Corps
H&S	Headquarters and Service	TAOR	Tactical area of responsibility
HE	High Explosive	T/O	Table of organization
HEAT	High Explosive Antitank	VC	Viet Cong
HEP-T	High Explosive Plastic Tracer	VT	variable time
HMM	Marine helicopter squadron	VTR	Vehicle, tank recovery
HUMINT	human intelligence	WP	White Phosphorous

Distances, ranges, and dimensions are mostly given in the contemporary US system of inches, feet, yards, and statute miles. A simple conversion table is provided below.

feet to meters:	multiply feet by 0.3048
yards to meters	multiply yards by 0.9114
miles to kilometers	multiply miles by 1.6093
centimeters to inches	multiply centimeters by 0.3937

Index

References to illustrations are shown in **bold**.